W9-DDN-506

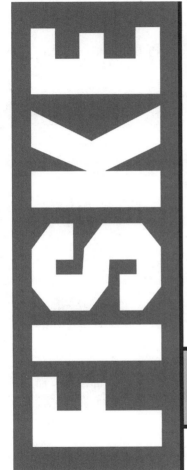

FISKE

WHAT
TO DO
WHEN

FOR COLLEGE

2006–2007

A Student and Parent's Guide to Deadlines, Planning and the Last Two Years of High School

EDWARD B. FISKE & BRUCE G. HAMMOND

SOURCEBOOKS, INC.®
NAPERVILLE, ILLINOIS

Published by Sourcebooks, Inc.
P.O. Box 4410, Naperville, Illinois 60567–4410
(630) 961–3900
Fax: (630) 961–2168
www.sourcebooks.com

ISBN-13:978-1-4022-0595-8
ISBN-10:1-4022-0595-3

Previous edition cataloged as follows:

Fiske, Edward B.
    Fiske what to do when for college, 2005/2006 : a week-by-week guide / by Edward B. Fiske and Bruce G. Hammond.
        p. cm.
    Rev. ed. of: Fiske college deadline planner, 2004-2005. c2003.
    Includes index.
    ISBN 1-4022-0307-1 (alk. paper)
    1.   Universities and colleges--United States--Admission--Calendars. 2. High school students--Scholarships, fellowships, etc.-- United States--Calendars. 3. Deadlines--United States. I. Title: What to do when for college, 2005/2006. II. Hammond, Bruce G. III. Fiske, Edward B. Fiske college deadline planner, 2004-2005. IV. Title.

    LB2351.2.F565 2004
    378.1'61--dc22

2004024394

Printed and bound in the United States of America
VG 10 9 8 7 6 5 4 3 2 1

To Andrea

and Sunny

CONTENTS

Deadlines, deadlines, deadlines. Life is full of them, but nowhere are deadlines more important than in college admission. The story is the same whether you're applying for admission, registering for standardized tests, or trying to win a scholarship: Find out the due date and get it there on time.

The main purpose of *Fiske What to Do When for College* is to help families stay on top of the welter of deadlines in college admission. The book follows key dates in the admission process week-by-week, but we recommend that you read it long before the crucial dates arrive. Meeting any deadline typically requires plenty of advance preparation.

Because the calendar is so crucial in college admission, we have built the entire book around dates and deadlines. We cover the process month-by-month and week-by-week from January 2006 through early April of 2007. The dates in this book are all national deadlines that fall mainly into several categories:

- **Standardized testing.** We have included the registration deadlines, late-registration deadlines, and test dates for the SAT and ACT through the spring of 2007. Most of these dates have already been announced by the test-makers.

- **Application deadlines.** Included are early-decision, early-action, regular-decision, and financial aid deadlines at major institutions. All such deadlines, unless otherwise noted, are for students in twelfth grade.

- **Institutional scholarship deadlines.** Many colleges have early deadlines for their major scholarships. We have listed all institutional scholarship deadlines at major institutions. Unless otherwise noted, scholarships are for current twelfth graders and are renewable for four years.

- **Portable scholarship and contest deadlines.** Private corporations and foundations offer portable scholarships and awards. They are portable because they can be used at any college. Unless otherwise noted, scholarships and contests are for twelfth graders.

Many of the dates, such as those for SAT and ACT testing, have already been announced through spring of 2007. Other dates, such as scholarship and admission deadlines, are subject to change. Therefore, **we recommend that you verify all admission and scholarship dates with the appropriate authority.** Where possible, the book includes Web links to allow you to do so with a few quick clicks.

> I wish I had started earlier with the whole college search process. It comes up quickly.
> —University of Michigan student

Various parts of the book will be more or less useful depending on whether you are in the Class of 2006, the Class of 2007, or a future class. In the winter and early spring, the application and scholarship deadlines generally apply to twelfth graders, while testing deadlines generally apply to eleventh graders. In the fall, most deadlines apply to twelfth graders. In general, scholarship competitions are available to twelfth graders only, while essay contests, science fairs, and other competitions with cash awards may be open to younger students.

Structure of the Book

The structure of this book is user-friendly and easy to follow. The format consists of the following:

Monthly overviews. These consist of brief summaries of the month's priorities, including a list of key dates called "What To Do." Use these dates as a quick guide to the most important stuff.

Weekly Calendar entries. This is your practical guide to the nuts and bolts of college planning, including details about scholarship programs, admission deadlines, testing deadlines, and every other date you can think of.

The Daily Planner. Every date through April of 2007 is listed. Use this as your college admission calendar. We hope that you will record your own personal appointments and due dates alongside those that are listed.

Advice Essays. Along with our What To Do commentary, we offer additional essays about various facets of the admission process. From planning college visits to prepping for the SAT, these include our best advice for every facet of the college search. We have placed these essays adjacent to the weeks and months of the calendar when the advice is most timely.

Quotes from Students, Parents, and Counselors. As part of our research for this book, we surveyed more than two hundred students and dozens of parents and counselors. The best of their advice is included in the bold quotations spread throughout the text. We chose "Counselor's heads-up" to denote advice from the guidance office, and to ensure the candor of our sources, we made these quotations anonymous. We identify students and parents by where they (or their sons and daughters) decided to attend college.

Appendices. What, you may ask, are appendices? The short answer is that the word "appendices" is the plural of appendix, which is a section that includes information that supplements the regular text. (Our hearty congratulations if you already knew all that.) Our appendices include lists of all the important dates in the book by category—SAT dates, ACT dates, admission and scholarship deadlines, and much more. For a complete list of what you'll find in the appendices, turn to the main contents or the mini contents on page 219.

> I've learned the hard way that a good essay and solid test scores can't always make up for a mediocre GPA.
>
> —Lewis & Clark College student

Since we know that the admission process is stressful, we have included a few additional items to lighten the mood. We hope you will enjoy the Student and Parent Pledges on pages xx and xxi as a light-hearted but serious reminder to keep both feet on the ground. With apologies to David Letterman, we also offer a few Top Five and Top Ten lists that we hope will both amuse and enlighten you.

TAKE A CHILL PILL, MOM AND DAD

This book is designed to be the savviest one yet on the nuts and bolts of getting into college. Our primary audience is eleventh and twelfth graders—with maybe a few on-the-ball tenth graders mixed in. We hope you will read through the book at the beginning of your college search, then refer to it again and again as key deadlines near.

We also hope that this book will be useful to parents, and we address many passages directly to them. Why include mom and dad? Let's do a reality check. Which person in your household is the one who reminds everyone else about approaching deadlines, who plans ahead months (or years) for every phase of the college search? If any students out there are nodding and pointing to themselves, we invite you to grab this book and get started. You have our permission to cut Mom and Dad out of the loop—with maybe an occasional update and some consultation about finances.

We're betting that most households work in a slightly different way, and we're not ready to put Mom and Dad out to pasture just yet. In most families, parents play an important role in the admission process. Parents, the balance is delicate: How can you grease the wheels without gumming up the works? Or, to change the metaphor, how can you pave the way without dictating the path? As long as you remember the fundamental truth about the college search—that it's all about the students—you can play a productive and even crucial role.

Letting go is hard, and it begins before the first college viewbook hits the mailbox. For parents accustomed to making decisions on behalf of their children, the college search is a new phase of life. Haltingly at first, but with growing confidence, students can emerge from the shadow of Mom and Dad as the process unfolds. Some parents think that because college is so important, they need to step in. When parents feel that urge coming on, the right response is often to step back.

> **Consider colleges that you've never heard of, including those with funny names.**
>
> **—Counselor's heads-up**

For students and parents alike, we offer the unvarnished truth about the college search—day-by-day, week-by-week. But keep this in mind: No college search will ever happen exactly on the timetable outlined here. Just because we cover it day-by-day does not mean you should be stressing about it day-by-day. Different dates will be relevant to different students. Use this book as a guideline, not as a blueprint for when everything must take place.

We are concerned that in many schools and many families, the college search has spun out of control. The pressures on today's applicants would have been unimaginable twenty years ago. From every corner of a student's universe, the message comes loud and clear that self-worth is synonymous with high SAT scores and college acceptance letters:

- High schools measure their own worth by which colleges their students get into and how many of these students have high test scores.

- Colleges tout themselves based on their selectivity and on the test scores and class rank of their entering class.

- Parents (some of them, anyway) act as if they will accept nothing less than a "name" school acceptable in their social circles.

High school students are not stupid. They absorb all these messages while the stakes keep getting higher. Meanwhile, admission gets tougher and tougher as the Baby Boom echo continues to work its way through the school system.

Compassionate parents must fight a guerrilla campaign against the idea that intellectual ability (and college admission) equals self-worth. Parents should praise their sons and daughters for something other than A's on the report card. Keep an

> My son was reluctant to go on college visits and almost had to be dragged to the schools we saw.
>
> —Lehigh University mom

open mind about colleges you may not have heard of. Teenagers should have the space to be teenagers. Assure them that wherever they choose go to college will be just fine.

Keeping It All in Perspective

The hysteria surrounding admission to the nation's most selective colleges has reached scary proportions. What is behind it? Some parents swear that getting into a prestigious college means a fast track to a plum job, a great career, and a rewarding life. The theory is interesting, but there is no evidence to support it. Undeniably, a high-brow diploma comes in handy in a student's first job interview. After that, one's alma mater doesn't mean much outside the cocktail party circuit.

Do lesser-known institutions have any advantages? You bet they do. Let's say a top student turns down Stanford and goes to Lawrence University in Appleton, Wisconsin, or enrolls in the honors program at Ohio University. Top students at places such as these will get some or all of the following:

- A merit scholarship

- Small classes with top faculty

- Research opportunities normally reserved for graduate students

- First shot at special summer opportunities

- Grooming for postgraduate fellowships

- Great graduate school recommendations from professors who really know them

- The satisfaction of being near the top rather than in the middle of the pack

Good luck on getting all this at Prestige U as another face in the glossy crowd.

> **Picking a college doesn't have to be voodoo. There are 2,200 four-year colleges in the country, and about 200 of them will be "right" for a student.**
>
> **—Counselor's heads-up**

We realize that many students will still want to play the highly selective college game. As graduates of Wesleyan and Yale, we will not try to dissuade anyone. Four years at a highly selective college can be an incredible experience for the right student. But the highly selective hysteria is not about having a good experience, getting a good education, or finding the right job. Rather, it is about recognition, self-image, and joining an exclusive club. There is nothing wrong with seeking distinction—everyone does

it. But let's be honest with ourselves about what is really at stake.

As the book unfolds, we poke fun at the hyper-anxiety that has taken over the college search. To keep pedantic lecturing to a minimum, we have summarized some of our most crucial themes in the Student's and Parent's College Admission Pledges that follow on pages xx and xxi. We hope you will laugh as you see a bit of yourself in our caricatures. We also hope families will read these together and discuss the themes we raise. The tone is light-hearted, but our message for parents is consistent: Keep your eye firmly on what is best for your son or daughter's long-term well-being.

There are a lot of desperately unhappy students enrolled at the Harvards of the world, and many more who are on their way to a happy and successful life attending colleges few people have ever heard of. Some students think that a void in their lives will be filled by a prestigious alma mater. They are sadly mistaken. What today's students really need is the absolute certainty that their parents will love and respect them no matter where they go to college. We urge students to look inside themselves for the qualities that do not depend on the verdict of an admission committee. It is those qualities, not an acceptance letter, that will sustain them as they go forward to begin a new stage in their life.

The college search often starts early—sometimes a little too early:

- A pregnant mother calls the local private school to put her son-to-be on the waiting list.

- The father of a two-year-old phones Harvard and Yale to find out the preferred preschool in his city for grooming an Ivy Leaguer.

- Parents pay hundreds of dollars for a consultant to coach their four-year-old for the high-stakes prekindergarten interview that will determine admission to primary school.

Although the rest of the country may roll its eyes, anecdotes like this are commonplace in Boston, New York, and other East Coast cities. Everybody is chasing the same prize, and the race starts early. There is nothing wrong with being ambitious, but we counsel parents to temper the stresses whenever possible.

Most parents reading this book have kids of high school age, but some of you may be planning ahead for younger ones. The following is a brief survey of dos and don'ts through the winter of eleventh grade. (Students should feel free to skip down to "Picking the Right Courses.")

Let Your Child Make Choices

Any good kindergarten teacher will tell you that children learn best in a stimulating environment where they are free to pursue their interests. The same applies to preparation for college. Parents do more harm than good when they try to mold their children into a preconceived notion of well-roundedness. Admission offices prefer students who are exceptionally good in one or two activities rather than reasonably good in ten. A detailed regimen of the "right" activities will only succeed in making your son or daughter just like everyone else's. Broad exposure is important, but so too is the freedom to pursue a few strong interests.

Don't Buy Your Child a Princeton Sweatshirt

Or, if your son or daughter already has a Princeton sweatshirt, find a place to tuck it away. Such things may seem innocent, but they carry a subtle message. The danger is most acute when Mom and Dad graduated from prestigious alma maters. Fewer than half of the high school valedictorians who apply to Princeton are admitted; how sad when preteens are saddled with those expectations. Many colleges now receive twice as many applications as they did in the 1970s and '80s, and even the adults who attended prestigious schools back then might not be admitted today. Even if your alma mater is not highly selective, tread lightly. Push too hard and your son or daughter just might push back.

> Help your child find the right fit: not your alma mater, not their friends' choice, but the place best suited to him or her.
>
> —Amherst College dad

The Pros and Cons of the National "Talent" Programs

The best-known national academic programs for elementary and middle schoolers are the self-styled "talent programs": the Center for Talented Youth at Johns Hopkins University (www.cty.jhu.edu); the Talent Identification Program at Duke University (www.tip.duke.edu); the Center for Talent Development at Northwestern University (www.ctd.northwestern.edu); and the Rocky Mountain Talent Search at University of Denver (www.du.edu/education/ces/rmts.html). These organizations divide the country regionally and offer enrichment programs for students through the elementary, middle, and early high school years. The talent programs identify potential applicants based on high test scores on school-administered standardized tests. Beginning in seventh grade, these programs give students the option of taking the SAT in order to qualify. Successful students earn recognition and attend summer programs on the campuses of the respective universities. Some critics argue that the talent programs introduce college-style pressure and competition to the middle grades, and that the SAT is better saved until high school. But some students say that taking the SAT at an early age helps raise their comfort level when they see it again in later years. As to the experience that these programs offer, most attendees give them a thumbs-up.

Picking the Right Courses

No matter what their age, students should take appropriately challenging courses—with an emphasis on the word "appropriately." Mental health (and grade point average) can suffer when students are overloaded. Under most circumstances, students should take a course every year in the core areas of English, history, math, science, and foreign language. But some students may not be cut out to take the honors track in every subject, or may want to devote more energy to arts or computer courses instead of taking Honors French III. A common parental mistake is to try to shoehorn their kids into the accelerated math track, often against the school's advice. If C's are the result, it won't help. For a peek ahead at what colleges look for in a high school curriculum, consult their websites or publications. For advice on picking courses for grade twelve, see page 39.

High School Activities: Quality over Quantity

Some high school students have the idea that sitting in the back of a few SADD meetings or getting inducted into the National Honor Society will make their college application stand out. Not so. Extracurricular activities and jobs are valuable

when they show one of the following: initiative, passion, leadership, or distinction. Unusual talents or activities are more interesting than run-of-the-mill ones, but don't count on a community service project in Kashmir to be the magic bullet. Colleges recognize that wealthy families have better access to fancy-schmancy programs in far-away places. Compelling qualities can also be shown close to home. Our advice to students: Do what you love, and stick with it.

> I have actually had a college call me and say, "Get your parents off of the phone!" If the parents call, the colleges immediately assume that the student is too lazy or stupid to pick up the phone and dial ten numbers.
>
> —Counselor's heads-up

The PSAT and PLAN

Many high schools administer the Preliminary SAT to students in October of tenth grade. Some schools also administer the PLAN, a pre-ACT, generally in fall of tenth grade. In eleventh grade, the vast majority of high schools administer the PSAT, and this time high scorers are eligible for recognition in the National Merit Scholarship

Program. (For details, see page 24.) Check with your guidance counselor to see when these tests are offered. If a school does not offer one or the other, students may arrange to take the test(s) at a school that does. These tests are valuable because they can help predict a student's SAT and ACT scores and help determine which one will offer them the best chance of scoring high. Families can also use scores from the PSAT or PLAN as a basis for considering an SAT or ACT prep course.

> It was hard not to nag in the beginning when I felt my son should be doing more. We gave him our suggestions for schools and topics for essays, but then had to step back and let him make the decisions.
>
> —Harvey Mudd College mom

Round One of the SAT

Among high school counselors, talking about the SAT for students younger than eleventh grade is a little like talking about bad breath. *Eeesh.* Nobody wants to feed the hype that is already rampant, or turn top students into stressed-out SAT weenies. But preparing for and/or taking the SAT in tenth grade may make sense for a few of the most advanced students. First, the math section of the SAT covers material that top students typically learn in ninth or tenth grade. When such students are questioned about taking the SAT, many say they suffered from being rusty on the math. Second, tenth grade is generally less stressful than eleventh, giving motivated students the time and energy to focus on the test. Lastly, strong students with a good shot at National Merit honors will probably want to do their prepping before taking the PSAT in October of eleventh grade. An SAT in May or June of tenth grade could make sense for some accelerated students, as could some prep for the SAT or PSAT in the summer after tenth grade. (For more on prep courses, see page 15.)

The SAT Subject Tests

SAT Subject Tests are hour-long tests in subjects such as writing, U.S. history, math, the sciences, and foreign language, twenty-one of them all told. SAT Subject Tests are required or recommended by a few dozen of the nation's most selective institutions. (For a complete list, see Appendix A.) Most students take the SAT Subject Tests beginning in June of eleventh grade, but an increasing number of early birds take them in tenth and even ninth grade. Such students are looking for an early read on how they can score, and want to reduce the pressure on themselves in eleventh grade. The Subject Tests are generally best taken at the end of a school year, after students have covered the material and while it is still fresh. Some intrepid ninth graders take the biology test, and chemistry is a likely choice for tenth graders. Accelerated math students taking precalculus or the equivalent in tenth grade may want to try the Math Level II exam. We recommend that only exceptionally strong students attempt subject tests before eleventh grade. Keep in mind that all Subject-Test scores are part of the student's testing record and will be reported to all colleges they apply to.

Students with Disabilities: Testing and Documentation

Students with physical and learning disabilities have the right to take college admission tests with appropriate accommodations, including extended time, large print, an audio version of the test, and so on. The scores of tests taken with accommodations such as these are no longer "flagged," so students should not hesitate. Schools file the paperwork, and the test-makers have two basic requirements for nonstandard testing:

- A diagnostic evaluation of the student and recommendation for extended time on the test by a qualified professional

- Evidence that the school has acknowledged the disability and is granting similar accommodations for that student in class

Families should initiate the approval process as soon as possible and no later than the beginning of tenth grade. Be aware that both the College Board and the ACT require diagnostic testing within the preceding three years to confirm the original evaluation. Both are also finicky about approving accommodations for students whose initial diagnosis comes within the context of the college admission process. If you've ever wondered about testing for your child, do it sooner rather than later.

> The flood of mail tends to make students think they are being sought after—and they may be—or maybe they are just being encouraged to apply to increase the application numbers.
>
> —Counselor's heads-up

Student's College Admission Pledge

I have accepted the fact that my parents are clueless. I am serene. I will betray not a tremor when they offer opinions or advice, no matter how laughable. My soul will be light as a feather when my mother elbows her way to the front of my college tour and talks the guide's ear off. I am serene.

Going to college is a stressful time for my parents, even though they are not the ones going. I recognize that neurosis is beyond anyone's control. Each week, I will calmly reassure them that I am working on my essays, have registered for my tests, am finishing my applications, have scheduled my interviews, am aware of all deadlines, and will have everything done in plenty of time. I will smile good-naturedly as my parent asks four follow-up questions at College Night.

I will try not to say no simply because my parents say yes, and remain open to the possibility, however improbable, that they may have a point. I may not be fully conscious of my anxieties about the college search—the fear of being judged and the fear of leaving home are both strong. I don't really want to get out of here as much as I say I do, and it is easier to put off thinking about the college search than to get it done. My parents are right about the importance of being proactive, even if they do get carried away.

Although the college search belongs to me, I pledge to listen to my parents. They know me better than anyone else, and they are the ones who will pay most of the bills. Their ideas about what will be best for me are based on years of experience in the real world. I will seriously consider what they say as I form my own opinions.

I must take charge of the college search. If I do, the nagging will stop and everyone's anxiety will go down. My parents have given me a remarkable gift—the ability to think and do for myself. I know I can do it with a little help from Mom and Dad.

Parent's College Admission Pledge

I am resigned to the fact that my child's college search will end in disaster. I am serene. Deadlines will be missed and scholarships will be lost as my child lounges under pulsating headphones or stares transfixed at a Game Cube. I accept the fact that I am a parent and therefore know nothing. I am serene.

Confronted with endless procrastination, my impulse is to take control—to register for tests, plan visits, schedule interviews, and get applications. It was I who asked those four follow-up questions at College Night—I couldn't help myself. And yet I know that everything will be fine if I can summon the fortitude to relax. My child is smart, capable, and perhaps a little too accustomed to me jumping in and fixing things. I will hold back. I pledge to drop hints and encourage, then back off. I will facilitate rather than dominate. The college search won't happen on my schedule, but it will happen.

I will not get too high or low about any facet of the college search. By doing so, I give it more importance than it really has. My child's self-worth may already be too wrapped up in getting an acceptance letter. I will attempt to lessen the fear rather than heighten it.

I will try not to say no simply because my son or daughter says yes, and I will remain open to the possibility, however improbable, that my child has the most important things under control. I understand that my anxiety comes partly from a sense of impending loss. I can feel my child slipping away. Sometimes I hold on too tightly or let social acceptability cloud the issue of what is best.

I realize that my child is almost ready to go and that a little rebellion at this time of life can be a good thing. I will respect and encourage independence, even if some of it is expressed as resentment toward me. I will make suggestions with care and try to avoid unnecessary confrontation.

Paying for college is my responsibility. I will take a major role in the search for financial aid and scholarships and speak honestly to my child about the financial realities we face.

I pledge to help my son or daughter take charge of the college search. I will try to support but not smother, encourage but not annoy, and consult but not control. The college search is too big to be handled alone—I will be there every step of the way.

Investigating the Academies

This applies only to students who think they may be cut out for attending the Army, Navy, Air Force, Coast Guard, or Merchant Marine academies. Interested students should begin exploring this option by the fall of eleventh grade. Candidates must generally be nominated to the academies by members of Congress, many of whom hold information nights for prospective students in the fall. Contact the office of your senator or representative. Application deadlines vary. Candidates are evaluated on the basis of academic achievement, leadership, and physical fitness. Interested students should consider attending one of the week-long summer programs held at the academies for a taste of the military lifestyle. (See noteworthy summer programs, page 90).

As long as I didn't mention my favorite school, my daughter would listen to me. But my personal favorite was completely rejected.

—Tufts University mom

I realized that the paperwork was a formidable task for a busy high school senior, and agreed to organize the process in terms of files, deadlines, and dealing with the volumes of mail.

—Yale University mom

It is important to lay the groundwork for a successful college search, but high school should not be reduced to a cram session for college. Too many teens arrive at college as burned-out survivors rather than eager learners. If thoughts of planning for college are dominating your life—or if your teen is showing signs of college stress—find ways to ease the tension and bring back a little joy.

Sometimes the best antidote for anxiety is information. The pages that follow detail all the twists and turns in the college admission process, week-by-week. For an extended discussion of the topics herein, pick up a copy of the *Fiske Guide to Getting into the Right College.*

JANUARY 2006

FOR THE CLASS OF 2006, regular-decision deadlines come thick and fast this month. Financial aid applications should be filed by the end of January. Students who have been knee-deep in the admission process can use this month to refocus on the scholarship search.

Eleventh graders should begin their college search in earnest this month and plan for visits over spring break. Now is also the time to think about a standardized test schedule for the spring. What combination of SAT, ACT, and the Subject Tests will you take? (For advice, see pages 49 and 83.) January is also a good time to give serious thought to summer travel plans.

WHAT TO DO:

✓ **Sunday, January 1**
Regular-decision deadlines at the most selective colleges

✓ **Friday, January 6**
February ACT registration deadline

✓ **Sunday, January 15**
Regular-decision deadlines at highly selective colleges

✓ **Saturday, January 28**
SAT and Subject Tests administered

January 1–7, 2006

For the Class of 2006, the new year brings a rush to the post office for the last-minute applicants to highly selective colleges. January 1 is the admission deadline at all eight of the Ivy League universities; at little Ivies such as **Amherst**, **Williams**, **Wesleyan**, and **Swarthmore**; and at the likes of **MIT**, **Caltech**, **Bucknell**, **Duke**, and **Northwestern**, to name a few. (With no mail service on New Year's Day, "January 1" really means "December 31," though a few schools, **Yale** among them, officially give students until January 2.) Early Decision (ED) II, a second round of binding commitment ED deadlines after those in November, arrives at places such as **Bates**, **Emory**, **Hobart and William Smith**, **Scripps**, **Swarthmore**, and **Washington U (MO)**. (For a complete list of January 1 deadlines, see Appendix B.)

January 1 is the first day that the FAFSA can be legally filed for students entering college in the fall of 2006. Chase down those W-2's and 1099's as fast as possible. For families who plan to file the FAFSA online, both student and parent should secure a PIN for their electronic signature as soon as possible at www.pin.ed.gov.

Most eleventh graders are dimly aware that they will one day go to college, and February is generally a good time for a first crack at the ACT. Students can then take the test a second time in April or June to have two scores in time for a possible early-decision or early-action application. The first fall date available nationwide is October, and while scores generally arrive in time for early consideration, you may not see them before the deadline.

Villanova strategically places its admission deadline for the weekend after New Year's. The **Discover Card Tribute Award** is one of the few recognition programs targeted solely at eleventh graders and is among the nation's most competitive, with nearly five hundred one-time awards of up to $25,000. The **JFK Essay Contest** also offers one-time scholarships of up to $3,000 to students in grades 9–12.

Sunday, January 1

☐ Application deadlines at the most selective colleges

☐ Early Decision II deadlines

☐ Institutional scholarship deadlines

☐ First day to file the Free Application for Federal Student Aid (FAFSA) for 2006–2007. www.fafsa.ed.gov

Monday, January 2

Tuesday, January 3

Wednesday, January 4

Thursday, January 5

Friday, January 6

☐ February ACT, registration deadline

Saturday, January 7

☐ Villanova University, admission deadline

☐ Discover Card Tribute Award. www.discovercard.com/tribute.htm

☐ JFK Profile in Courage Essay Contest. www.jfkcontest.org

January 8–14, 2006

January 15 has traditionally been the second date circled in red on the calendar of regular-decision deadlines, but a growing number of institutions now use January 10. The January 10 list includes **Cooper Union** (art only), **Elon, Georgetown, Occidental, Rice**, and **University of Southern California**.

Seniors should seek out their guidance counselors to make sure that transcripts and recommendations have been forwarded to all colleges. Midyear grades will be sent in the next several weeks, and students should alert their counselors to any new awards or other information that could be included in the report (such as your recent selection to the all-district volleyball team). In cases where you have personally met an admission officer (AO), it would be a nice touch to send an email letting the AO know that the application is on its way.

The **Ron Brown Scholar Program,** with a deadline of January 9, is the nation's most competitive for African Americans. In a recent year, there were 8,500 applications for the twenty scholarships offering a four-year total of $40,000. The Elks MVS offers five hundred renewable awards of up to $15,000 per year, and financial need is a factor. The **United Nations Association National High School Essay Contest** offers three awards of up to $3,000 and is open to students in grades 9–12.

For eleventh graders, the first two weeks of January is the traditional time for a school-sponsored College Night to kickoff or continue the college search. Mom sits in the front row, feverishly taking notes and asking questions; you sit in the back, giggling with friends and sinking lower in your seat every time Mom's hand goes up. So much for College Search 101.

Sunday, January 8

Monday, January 9

☐ Ron Brown Scholar Program. African Americans.
www.ronbrown.org

Tuesday, January 10

☐ Application deadlines at highly selective colleges

Wednesday, January 11

Thursday, January 12

Friday, January 13

☐ Elks Most Valuable Student Scholarship.
www.elks.org/enf/scholars/mvs.cfm

☐ United Nations Association National High School
Essay Contest. www.unausa.org

Saturday, January 14

January 15–21, 2006

The hit parade of highly selective colleges with January 15 admission deadlines includes **Colorado College, Emory, George Washington, Oberlin, Reed, Trinity (CT)**, and many more. Early Decision (ED) II, a second round of binding-commitment deadlines, is mainly the domain of small private colleges. Among those with January 15 ED II deadlines are **Carleton, Colgate, Denison, Drew, Skidmore**, and **Wheaton (MA)**.

The nation's premier scholarship for minority students—the **Gates Millennium**—offers more than one thousand renewable full-ride scholarships to those with high financial need. The **Phi Delta Kappa Scholarship** offers one-time scholarships up to $5,000 to prospective education majors, and the **Department of Agriculture 1890 Scholarship** offers full-ride renewable awards to students looking at historically black colleges. The **Young Naturalist Awards** program gives one-time prizes of up to $2,500 to students in grades 7–12 for outstanding science projects in biology, earth science, or astronomy. (YNA is sponsored by the American Museum of Natural History.) Open to students in grades 7–12, the **DuPont Challenge** requires an essay of not more than one thousand words on a scientific topic for one-time scholarships up to $1,500. The intensely competitive **National Honor Society** (NHS) scholarship offers two hundred one-time awards of $1,000. A school nomination is required. The **Telluride Association** sponsors two of the nation's elite summer programs in the humanities. A program for eleventh graders (deadline January 16) is open to all, while one for tenth graders is open to minority students. Both are free.

In the middle of January, summer vacation can seem light-years away to a stressed-out eleventh grader—good thing Mom and Dad are there for a gentle reminder. Now is the time to think seriously about summer.

Sunday, January 15

- ☐ Application deadlines at highly selective colleges Early Decision II deadlines at moderately selective colleges
- ☐ Gates Millennium Scholarship. www.gmsp.org
- ☐ Phi Delta Kappa International Scholarship. www.pdkintl.org

- ☐ USDA 1890 National Scholars Program. 1890scholars.program.usda.gov
- ☐ Young Naturalist Awards. www.amnh.org/nationalcenter/ youngnaturalistawards

Monday, January 16

☐ Telluride Association Summer Programs, 10th Grade.
www.tellurideassociation.org

_____

_____

Tuesday, January 17

_____

_____

_____

_____

Wednesday, January 18

_____

_____

Thursday, January 19

_____

_____

Friday, January 20

☐ Grinnell College, University of Maryland,
University of Rochester, admission deadline

☐ National Honor Society Scholarship. www.nhs.us

_____

_____

Saturday, January 21

_____

_____

_____

_____

If your college fund is in tatters and finding a spare $150,000 is not an option, get set for a dose of reality. You may not be able to afford your dream school. Twenty years ago, we would have told you to take a deep breath and wait for the need-based aid. But with tuition up, grants down, and middle-income families feeling the heat, the financial bottom line cannot be ignored.

> I believe that students should have a certain arrogance when applying to colleges—meaning that you should have confidence in what you've done in your previous three years and know that whatever happens, happens.
>
> —Duke University student

Is Dream U out of reach? It is too early to know in January of eleventh grade, but this month is a perfect time for families to sit down and go over the financial parameters of the college search. Do it now—before anybody gets his or her heart set on a school that may not be realistic.

Some parents hem and haw, avoid the issue, and then pull the rug out in April of twelfth grade. Parents, the time is now to put your cards on the table—just because you may not be able to afford some colleges doesn't make you a bad parent. Expensive is not always better. Have a candid conversation about the role that finances may play. Don't eliminate Dream U—you never know what scholarships or aid may come down the pike—but help your child hedge his or her bets by identifying options that are likely to be less expensive. Here are some strategies:

- **Investigate need-based aid**. Go to www.collegeboard.com and click on "Paying for College" and then "How Much Will Your Family Have to Pay?" There, you'll find a program that will estimate your ability to qualify for aid. Better still, go ahead and file this year's Free Application for Federal Student Aid (FAFSA) even though your student is only an eleventh grader. You won't actually get money because your child will still be in high school in 2005–2006, but the report you get back will tell you how much you would be expected to pay for college.

• **Target a Merit Scholarship**. Encourage your son or daughter to identify schools where a merit scholarship might be in the cards. The best bet: colleges where the student would rank high in the applicant pool. A merit scholarship search can uncover gems that offer the benefits of being a big fish in a small pond.

Always fill out the information cards even if you know you are already on the college's mailing list. Never miss an opportunity to get an official "contact" in the computer system.

—Counselor's heads-up

• **Look for Bargains**. Every year, the *Fiske Guide to Colleges* lists the nation's best bargains, and the *Fiske Guide to Getting into the Right College* has a guide to budget options. In-state colleges are generally less expensive, and many states have reciprocity agreements with institutions in neighboring states. As an example, students in thirteen Western states can get reduced tuition at participating institutions in the other states under the Western Undergraduate Exchange.

The final decision of where to go should always belong to the student. Though parents may set financial limits, there are many outstanding colleges within any reasonable economic parameters.

Which summer activities look good on a college application? The kind where students can show initiative and independence while furthering an interest that will be reinforced by other parts of their application. Page one of the standard playbook is a summer program at a college or university. A summer on campus is a dry run for the real thing. Students get to sample dorm life, interact with real professors, and learn the importance of time management. The major negative to summer study is that students don't get a break from academics. Worst case scenario, students will go straight from their summer exams to the beginning of regular school.

Many people overestimate the extent to which a summer on campus will give students a leg up in

> I found that I was talking too much about the college process and adding stress to an already stressful situation. Once I stepped back and let my daughter take charge, things went more smoothly.
>
> —Knox College mom

the regular admission process. Colleges use summer programs to make money from facilities that would otherwise be idle. As long as the family is forking over $1,000-plus per week, they are not overly picky about who gets in. Even Harvard will admit almost any student with good grades and supportive recommendations. Going to a university summer program won't mean much in the real admission process, with the following exceptions:

- The student has middling grades and uses the summer to show that he or she is capable of college-level work.

- The student works closely with a professor who can write a strong letter of recommendation.

One other option that can cost a pretty penny is summer abroad. It can be a great opportunity, especially when you are reinforcing language skills or other interests. Better still: a summer of service abroad with programs such as Amigos de las Americas (www.amigoslink.org) or

The Experiment in International Living (www. usexperiment.org).

While a big-money summer program can be a great experience, there are plenty of other worthy options that won't cost the equivalent of a year's tuition at a state university. They include:

- Volunteer work
- Employment, preferably with the chance for leadership and responsibility
- An internship, paying or nonpaying, in a profession of interest

When in doubt, remember: initiative and independence. Better to start something than plug into somebody else's program, and better to show some imagination than follow the well-worn path.

> Girls are getting the shaft in college admission because of the imbalance of males to females on many college campuses. This is an important issue that no one is discussing openly.
>
> —Counselor's heads-up

January 22–28, 2006

January is the time for eleventh graders to get serious about their testing schedules. A few early birds will have already taken an SAT in the fall, but we recommend that ambitious students consider their first SAT in either January or March with a second round in May or June. If this planner had started in December, we would have noted that December 22 was the registration deadline for the SAT on January 28. For an extra $36, students who have not registered in advance can take the test as a standby by simply showing up at a test center with a completed registration form and a check in hand. Some test centers run out of room, so consult the College Board's list of centers, choose a likely one, and call the testing coordinator early in the week of the test to find out if they will have space. Standbys are always the last to get seated, but the process usually works.

The deadline for the **Telluride Association's** prestigious summer program for eleventh graders is this week.

Sunday, January 22

Monday, January 23

☐ Telluride Association Summer Program, 11th graders. www.tellurideassociation.org

Tuesday, January 24

Wednesday, January 25

Thursday, January 26

Friday, January 27

Saturday, January 28

☐ SAT and Subject Tests administered

JANUARY 29–31, 2006

The days of January typically find the parents of twelfth graders pulling their hair out at www.fafsa.ed.gov. In the early days of the Internet, the site was a disaster of lost data, broken links, and endless waiting for pages to load. Many of the bugs have been fixed (knock on wood) and filing the FAFSA online is now the preferred method. Using the electronic version catches common mistakes and speeds processing at a time when every day counts. Ideally, you'll file on the basis of a completed 2005 tax form. In the real world, many parents file the FAFSA (and CSS PROFILE) on the basis of estimated income figures. On the downside, filing on estimates increases the likelihood that you will be selected for verification—the equivalent of an audit. Plus, if you are off by more than $400 in your estimates, you'll need to file a correction. If you do file the FAFSA online, you are advised to check your status a week after doing so.

    Miami of Ohio chooses to live on the edge with a January 31 application deadline—as opposed to the more conventional February 1. **Papa John's Pizza** offers more than one thousand one-time scholarships of $1,000 to students who live in their delivery areas. **Navy ROTC** offers renewable full tuition and books at approximately 150 participating universities in exchange for a commitment to serve after graduation.

Sunday, January 29

_____

_____

Monday, January 30

_____

_____

Tuesday, January 31

☐ Miami University (OH), application deadline

☐ Papa John's Scholars.
  www.papajohnsscholars.com

☐ Navy ROTC Scholarship. www.todaysmilitary.com

_____

THE TRUTH ABOUT TEST PREP

Remember what your mom told you about stuff that sounds too good to be true? (Hint: It probably is.) Chalk up standardized test prep as one of those topics. To hear the test prep companies tell it, all you have to do is fork over a few hundred dollars (well, maybe $1,000) to get an eye-popping score increase on the SAT—guaranteed! To investigate those claims, we did a survey of more than 800 students at 70 schools who had taken the SAT. We found that those students who did not take a prep course actually scored higher than those who did. Hmm.

Are we suggesting that preparing for standardized tests is useless? Hardly. Hundreds of students told us in their surveys that the key to beating the SAT is taking timed practice tests—not listening to lectures about the SAT, not talking about it with a tutor, but practicing real questions under real conditions and then analyzing their results. Our recent book, *Fiske Nailing the New SAT*, goes over our survey and gives our best advice on how to prepare for the SAT. We recommend a similar approach for the ACT and the SAT Subject Tests.

Of course, there are some instances when paying for test prep may be the right choice. Likely candidates for a prep course include:

- Students who need adult direction
- Students who need the structure of a course to stay focused
- Students who are enthusiastic and will do the homework

Student enthusiasm is the most important indicator of these. If a student must be dragged kicking and screaming into the course, the odds of success are low. When there is a choice, go for one-on-one tutoring, even if it is only for a few sessions, rather than a one-size-fits-all course. The latter are often useless except for the practice tests. Pay no attention to score-increase guarantees. The fine print usually says that you won't get your money back, but you will be treated to a second helping of what didn't work the first time. The most important part of an SAT prep course is the instructor, not the brand name on the door. If you're convinced that paying for test prep is the right move, find a tutor you can connect with and give it your best shot.

THE STANDARDIZED TESTING MONEY MACHINE

The College Board owns the SAT. Educational Testing Service (ETS) produces and administers it. Together, they take in hundreds of millions of dollars every year on the test. Watch your wallet. The standard fee for the new SAT is $41.50, but miss a registration deadline and the price jumps to $62.50 for late registration and $77.50 to take it as a standby. Want to send scores to the colleges? College Board and ETS let you have four freebies at the time of registration, but if students want to see their scores before they send them, or they're not sure where they want to send the scores at the time they test, additional reports cost $9 per college. In a hurry? That's not good—the usual additional score-report procedure can take up to a month. But for only $26 extra (plus $9 per report), students can have their scores rushed in just two business days.

ACT operates from basically the same playbook, but with one major difference. Reporting all SAT and Subject Test results is cumulative—when you send a score, all your previous SAT and Subject Test scores are also sent. But with ACT, students can choose to send the scores from a particular date without sending the others. That idea is appealing to students and parents, but the downside is that students must pay for even more score reports.

Some high schools have helped families save a few bucks by putting test scores on the back of student transcripts. While many colleges have always held out for the "official" scores, others have taken scores from transcripts in lieu of receiving them directly from the test-makers. But this little racket may be on its last legs. Both the SAT and ACT now have an essay, and as each will be scanned into a computer, colleges can electronically access what students write. However, colleges have online access to those student essays only when students send their scores to the colleges through the College Board. (See page 42 for more on the new SAT.)

To avoid unnecessary fees that can run into hundreds of dollars, stay on top of registration and score-reporting deadlines.

HITTING THE GROUND RUNNING

This book lists dozens of scholarships and contests, most of which have fixed deadlines. The contests below have deadlines that vary by region, or have deadlines for local competitions that are a prelude to regional and national competitions. All are among the most prestigious competitions of their kind in the nation, and all can be entered by high schoolers of any age. Those who win in twelfth grade typically enter in the lower grades to hone their skills.

Scholastic Art and Writing Awards (grades 7–12). With 250,000 entries and 900 awards, SAWA is one of the largest student contests in the nation. Winners in twelfth grade are eligible for scholarships. Most deadlines are in January but vary by region of residence (www.scholastic.com/artandwritingawards).

National History Day (6–12). State contests are typically held in March, and winners advance to National History Day in June. Nine one-time scholarships of up to $1,000 are awarded (www.nationalhistoryday.org).

American Legion's National High School Oratorical Contest (9–12). Deadlines vary by state but are usually in winter. Offers one-time scholarships of up to $18,000 (www.legion.org).

Intel Science and Engineering Fair (9–12). An umbrella organization for five hundred regional science fairs generally held in March. Winners compete in the national fair in May for one-time scholarships of up to $50,000. Nearly five hundred fairs worldwide (www.sciserv.org/isef).

Junior Science and Humanities Symposium (9–12). Regional symposia in early spring showcase original research projects in math, science, and engineering. National symposium in May. Forty-eight one-time scholarships of up to $20,000 (www.jshs.org).

United States Senate Youth Program (11–12). Two winners per state get a week in Washington, D.C., and a one-time $5,000 scholarship. To be eligible, students must serve in elected office and be nominated by a school official or state-level administrator. Deadlines vary by state (www.hearstfdn.org/ussyp).

FEBRUARY 2006

WITH COLLEGE APPLICATIONS FINALLY out the door, the February blahs should be no big deal for the Class of 2006. Students are advised to log onto colleges' websites to make sure their applications are complete. Most financial aid deadlines arrive this month. Financial aid filers should watch for correspondence through the mail (paper filers) or online (electronic filers). Verify that your information is correct. Families with special financial circumstances should contact the colleges directly. (See page 185.)

Members of the Class of 2007 should continue researching colleges and meet with their college counselors if possible. Register for the April SAT and/or the April ACT where applicable. Families should solidify plans for college visits during spring break and continue weighing summer options.

WHAT TO DO:

✓ **Wednesday, February 1**
Application deadlines at moderately selective colleges
Financial aid deadlines at highly selective colleges

✓ **Wednesday, February 15**
Application deadlines at moderately selective colleges

✓ **Friday, February 24**
April SAT, registration deadline

FEBRUARY 1–4, 2006

A slew of colleges have February 1 application deadlines, including **American, Franklin and Marshall, Rhodes, University of San Francisco, University of Texas at Austin, University of Wisconsin at Madison,** and **Wofford**. February 1 is also D-Day for financial aid applications at highly selective institutions. (For a complete list of February 1 deadlines, see Appendix B.)

For raw numbers of scholarships, the **Sam Walton Community Scholarship** (of Wal-Mart fame) is probably the nation's largest, offering more than six thousand one-time awards of up to $25,000. Local winners have the chance to continue in the competition for scholarships totaling $25,000. **The Jaycees**, the Junior Chamber of Commerce, offer twenty-five one-time scholarships of $1,000, with leadership and financial need among the criteria. **Junior Achievement**, an organization that promotes business and economic literacy in schools, awards a range of scholarships with February 1 deadlines. **DAR** (Daughters of the American Revolution) also offers a range of scholarships related to U.S. history, government, economics, historic preservation, and health professions. (Various deadlines begin February 1.) **Toshiba** teams up with the **National Science Teachers Association** to offer a contest for kids of all ages who work in teams to design "technology of the future" for one-time awards of up to $10,000. The **National Peace Essay Contest** is one of the best known of its kind, with more than fifty one-time scholarships of up to $10,000.

Although most college summer programs are simply a vehicle for getting paying customers through the door, MIT is a conspicuous exception. Its **Research Science Institute** is a small, elite program that attracts some of the nation's top technically oriented students. (The program recently expanded to include an additional session at Caltech.) The same is true of **Minority Introduction to Engineering, Entrepreneurship, and Science**, a program for minority students and disadvantaged non-minorities. The **Women's Technology Program** is a magnet for the nation's top female students. It costs $2,000 for four weeks, but unlike many summer programs, the WTP provides generous need-based financial aid. All three programs are open to students in the summer after eleventh grade. (See Summer for Free, page 90.)

Wednesday, February 1

☐ Application deadlines at moderately selective colleges

☐ Financial aid deadlines at highly selective private colleges

☐ Jaycee War Memorial Fund Scholarship. www.usjaycees.org/scholarships.htm

☐ Sam Walton Community Scholarship. www.walmartfoundation.org

☐ Junior Achievement Scholarships. www.ja.org

☐ DAR Scholarships. www.dar.org

☐ National Peace Essay Contest. www.usip.org/ed/npec/index.html

☐ Toshiba/NSTA ExploraVision Awards. www.exploravision.org

☐ Research Science Institute Deadline. www.cee.org/rsi

☐ Women's Technology Program Deadline. wtp.mit.edu

Thursday, February 2

Friday, February 3

☐ Announcement of National Merit Finalists

☐ MIT Minority Introduction to Engineering, Entrepreneurship, and Science Summer Program. web.mit.edu/mites/www

Saturday, February 4

FEBRUARY 5–11, 2006

Mid-February is one of the toughest times of the school year for everyone. The weather is still bad, half the students are generally sick, and spring break is still nowhere in sight. Fortunately, the week is a light one for deadlines. The **American Foreign Service Association** offers merit awards of up to $2,500 and need-based awards up to $3,500, as well as an award for the best essay in its competition. For the Class of 2007, this week's ACT is the first of three available before the end of the school year.

Sunday, February 5

☐ American Foreign Service Association Scholarship.
www.afsa.org

Monday, February 6

Tuesday, February 7

Wednesday, February 8

_____   _____

_____   _____

_____   _____

Thursday, February 9

_____   _____

_____   _____

_____   _____

Friday, February 10

_____   _____

_____   _____

_____   _____

Saturday, February 11

☐ ACT Administered   _____

_____   _____

_____   _____

_____   _____

People in places like Connecticut, Massachusetts, and New Jersey are forever complaining that they get the shaft in college admission, and when it comes to the National Merit Program, they're right.

The PSAT, and in particular the one students take in eleventh grade, is the qualifying test for the National Merit Program. About 3 percent of the eleventh grade test-takers are designated as Commended Students and receive a certificate for their efforts. The top 1.25 percent of test-takers, more or less, are designated as National Merit Semifinalists.

But back to Connecticut, Massachusetts, and New Jersey. Since National Merit mandates a fixed number of winners in each state that is proportional to its population, these states have much higher qualifying scores than places like South Dakota or Wyoming. In Massachusetts, the qualifying Selection Index (SI) score for Semifinalists varies from year to year, but is usually about 221 (SI = verbal score + math score + writing skills score). In Wyoming, the qualifying score is about 201. (If the thought of moving to Wyoming suddenly sounds appealing, see Top Ten Signs that Mom and Dad Are Losing It, page 33.)

Once the Semifinalists are announced—in September of twelfth grade—they have about a month to write an essay and complete a short application, which is coupled with a counselor recommendation. Advancing to Finalist is a snap as long as your grades are in the A range. About 90 percent of Semifinalists become Finalists when the new crop is announced in early February. From here, the highest scorers are awarded one-time scholarships from National Merit of up to $2,500. Major corporations also make awards, usually to Finalists who are dependents of their employees or residents of areas where they operate. About two hundred four-year colleges offer scholarships to Finalists, including some institutions that make a cottage industry of enrolling Finalists with full-ride scholarships. (Don't count on anything but a yawn from Ivy-caliber schools, which are overrun with applications from National Merit honorees.)

In all, just over half of Finalists receive a scholarship. Whether or not Finalists get money may have less to do with merit than where they choose to go to college, where they live, and where their parents work.

CONGRATULATIONS! YOU'RE A LUCKY WINNER!

Most people have seen the banner ads on the Internet that say, "If flashing, you're a winner!" Funny how those banners are always flashing.

The same thing happens in college admission. College applicants and their parents are particularly vulnerable to the congratulations-you've-won-something ploy. Take Who's Who among American High School Students, an official-sounding outfit that has been "honoring" students since 1967. Exactly how students are chosen for this great honor is not entirely clear. One way or

> I urge students to choose one or two extracurriculars where they can make a real contribution rather than doing lots of insignificant ones.
>
> —Counselor's heads-up

another, Who's Who gets names and addresses from educational and civic organizations. One high school counselor tells us that she herself got a Who's Who nomination, apparently as a result of doing a scholarship search on www.fastweb.com.

The game at Who's Who is simple: In exchange for seeing your son or daughter's name in tiny type, they hope you'll buy a copy of their weighty, hardcover tome. What is a listing in Who's Who worth on a college application? Not much more than a sigh and a roll of the eyes.

> We had to insist that our son visit a couple of schools he hadn't considered. One of them ended up being one of his two final choices.
>
> —University of San Diego mom

FEBRUARY 12–18, 2006

Institutions with February 15 application deadlines include private colleges such as **Drew, Gettysburg, Rollins,** and **College of Wooster,** and public universities such as **University of Kentucky** and **State University of New York at Stony Brook**. (For a complete list, see Appendix B.) Any family that plans to file an application for financial aid—no matter what the institution—is advised to do so by February 15.

The **EF Global Citizen Essay Contest** offers twelve one-time scholarships of $1,000 and a ten-day trip to Europe. A school nomination is required. The **National Alliance for Scholastic Achievement** emphasizes academic excellence in awarding its five one-time scholarships of up to $15,000.

Sunday, February 12

_____

_____

_____

_____

Monday, February 13

_____

_____

_____

_____

Tuesday, February 14

_____

_____

_____

Wednesday, February 15

- ☐ Application deadlines at moderately selective colleges
- ☐ Financial aid deadlines at moderately selective private colleges and public universities

☐ EF Global Citizen Essay Contest. School nomination required. www.eftours.com

Thursday, February 16

Friday, February 17

- ☐ National Alliance for Scholastic Achievement Scholarship. www.eee.org/bus/nasa

Saturday, February 18

FEBRUARY 19–25, 2005

This week, financial aid filers are advised to make sure that their applications are on track. By now, families should have received a copy of the FAFSA student aid report (SAR) and a similar document from the CSS/PROFILE, either electronically or through the mail. (Snail-mail filers be aware that the SAR will come addressed to the student.) If there are special circumstances surrounding the aid application—such as a blip in income or unusual expenses or debts—write a letter directly to the financial aid office of every college where you are applying.

The **All-USA High School Academic Team** provides one-time awards of $2,500 to twenty students nominated by their schools.

Sunday, February 19

Monday, February 20

☐ All-USA High School Academic Team. School nomination required.
www.usatoday.com

Tuesday, February 21

Wednesday, February 22

_____   _____
_____   _____
_____   _____

Thursday, February 23

_____   _____
_____   _____
_____   _____

Friday, February 24

☐ April SAT registration deadline   _____
_____   _____
_____   _____

Saturday, February 25

_____   _____
_____   _____
_____   _____

FEBRUARY 26-28, 2006

The end of February can be the most depressing time of the school year. Winter is still hanging on, and spring break is weeks away. There could be no better time for the **Optimist International Essay Contest**, open to students in grades 9–12, which features one-time scholarships up to $5,000. The February 28 deadline is for the national contest; check with local Optimist Clubs for entry procedures. For a mere $200 registration fee, the **Girls' Leadership Workshop** offers nine days of programming at Val-Kill, the one-time rural getaway cottage of Eleanor Roosevelt, who is the inspiration for the program.

Sunday, February 26

Monday, February 27

Tuesday, February 28

☐ Queens College (CAN), admission deadline

☐ Optimist International Essay Contest.
www.optimist.org

☐ Girls' Leadership Workshop at Val-Kill,
application deadline.
www.ervk.org

COLLEGE ESSAYS: WINDOW ON THE SOUL OR JUST PLAIN WACKY?

When it comes to college essay topics, one never knows what the admission office will dream up. A recent topic at the University of Chicago was (we kid you not) "How do you feel about Wednesday?" Go figure. For years, Penn has asked the following mind-bender: "You have just completed your 300-page autobiography. Please submit page 217."

No wonder students dread these essays. The fact that many topics are straightforward is small consolation to the thousands of students who will soon enter a struggle to the death with one or more of them.

So why bring this up now? These essay questions are typical of the kind of reflectiveness the college search demands but that does not come naturally to many students. Some college counselors ask students to respond to essay questions while still in eleventh grade, not only to work on the writing process, but also to encourage a habit of thinking that will serve them well throughout the college process. Here are a few distinctive questions that have been used in recent years:

Chances are good that you're going to have one or more roommates at some point in your college years. What sort of person would make a good match for you? Explain why.

—Princeton University

Pearl Buck once said, "You cannot make yourself feel something you do not feel, but you can make yourself do right in spite of your feelings." Tell us about an experience where you felt that you "did the right thing" in spite of your feelings.

—Randolph-Macon Woman's College

If I could change the world, I would . . .

—University of Tulsa

Tell us about an opinion that you have had to defend or an incident in your life which placed you in conflict with the beliefs of a majority of people and explain how this affected your value system.

—MIT

Fortunately, most colleges let students have a choice of which questions they want to answer, and many simply ask students to write about a topic that is meaningful to them. But grappling with questions like these is a good exercise, whether or not the particular colleges are on your list.

PLANNING A SPRING COLLEGE VISIT

For eleventh graders, February is an ideal time to think about the possibility of college visits during spring break. Such visits can be better than those in the summer because college spring break tends to be earlier than the break for high schools, and therefore college classes may be in session. Although the admission office will be preoccupied with last year's class—and perks such as a night in the dorms are generally available only for twelfth graders—the plusses outweigh the minuses.

A parent's first impulse may be to grab the phone and call the college. Good thought, but slow down. The student should make the call while mom and dad cool their heels. As we never tire of pointing out, the college admission process is all about the student taking control. Besides, a few colleges will even track whether it was the student or you who made the call. (Nothing personal, but they prefer to hear from students.)

Although students may tremble at the thought of calling an admission office, the procedure is easy: Dial the phone, say you're an eleventh grader looking at colleges, say the date you're coming, and then ask about the possibility of a) a tour, b) a group information session, c) an interview, and d) contact with someone in a department or program of interest. The person on the other end of the line will have heard these requests a thousand times (and will likely be an administrative assistant who will not be involved in evaluating your application). A tour is the only sure thing, but students should find out how much of the rest is available. Small colleges are more likely to offer the personal touch than big universities, which usually don't offer campus interviews.

A spring break visit is often a student's first real engagement with the college search. Parents can help by encouraging their son or daughter to take the lead.

TOP TEN SIGNS THAT MOM AND DAD ARE LOSING IT

Call it Pre-College Stress Syndrome: the debilitating illness that causes Mom and Dad to take leave of their senses for months at a time. Parents may be suffering from PCSS if they:

10. Attend eleventh-grade college night while son is still in middle school.

9. Propose *Fiske Guide to Colleges* as their book club's selection of the month.

8. Put the high school college counselor's home phone number on speed dial.

7. Dig out old report cards to calculate daughter's GPA to .0001 accuracy.

6. Revive friendship with obnoxious in-law who graduated from Duke.

5. Send flowers to phone receptionists at Amherst, Wesleyan, and Carleton.

4. House-hunt in Wyoming to enhance child's "geo" appeal at the Ivies.

3. Tell friends that "we" are applying to Stanford and Berkeley.

2. Wake up daughter each morning with CD of Ivy League fight songs.

1. Put vanity license plates reading "730V/770M" on the family S.U.V.

If any these sound familiar, have Mom and Dad reread the Parent's College Admission Pledge on page xxi.

MARCH 2006

Waiting really is the hardest part—just ask any college applicant. A few stray decision letters will arrive by early March, but most will not come until the last two weeks of the month. Families should scrutinize aid packages and make plans for a last round of college visits in April. Applicants to public institutions should keep a close eye on the procedures for getting a dorm room.

Juniors should use spring break for college visits and/or to prepare for standardized tests. Students in AP courses should make sure they are registered to take the exams.

WHAT TO DO:

✓ **Wednesday, March 1**
Application and financial aid deadlines at moderately selective colleges

✓ **Friday, March 3**
April ACT, registration deadline

✓ **Wednesday, March 15**
Application deadlines at moderately selective colleges

March 1–4, 2006

March 1 brings another spate of admission deadlines at moderately selective institutions, including **Albion College, Florida State University, Ithaca College, Lake Forest College, University of Oregon, Rose-Hulman Institute,** and **Susquehanna University**. (For a complete list of March 1 deadlines, see Appendix B.) For the Class of 2007, the April ACT date is the preferred spring alternative at many high schools, though some students decide to wait until June when school is out in much of the country.

Kaplan's "My Turn" Essay Contest gives entrants in grades 9–12 a shot at seeing their work in Newsweek's feature by the same name along with a one-time award of up to $5,000. The **Pfizer Epilepsy Scholarship Award**, offering one-time stipends up to $3,000, is among the most prominent awards available to students with a particular medical condition. The **Donna Reed Performing Arts Scholarships** include ten one-time awards of up to $4,000 for students who excel in acting, vocal music, and musical theater. The **Sons of the American Revolution** sponsor the Rumbaugh Oration Contest, open to students in grades 10-12, which requires students to do a 5-6 minute oration related to the Revolution for scholarships up to $3,000.

Carleton College offers one of the nation's premier summer programs for minority students, the Liberal Arts Experience. The program is open to students between tenth and eleventh grade. The program is one week long and the college pays all expenses, including travel. (See Summer for Free, page 90.) March 1 is

Wednesday, March 1

- ☐ Admission and financial aid deadlines at moderately selective institutions
- ☐ Kaplan/Newsweek "My Turn" Essay Contest. www.kaptest.com/essay
- ☐ Pfizer Epilepsy Scholarship Award. www.epilepsy-scholarship.com
- ☐ Donna Reed Performing Arts Scholarships. www.donnareed.org
- ☐ SAR Rumbaugh Oration Contest. www.sar.org
- ☐ Carleton Liberal Arts Experience Summer Program. www.carleton.edu/admissions/CLAE

Thursday, March 2

_____

_____

_____

Friday, March 3

☐ April ACT, registration deadline

_____

_____

Saturday, March 4

_____

_____

_____

_____

_____

_____

FOR PARENTS: SINGIN' THOSE PROCRASTINATION BLUES

There is no better symbol for the agonies of the college search than the tormented mother, unable to get her wayward son to think about where to go or what to study. (Daughters are also capable of procrastination, but sons are the undisputed champs.)

Why do these otherwise fine young men give their mothers such grief? Malice? Perverse sense of humor? Repressed conflicts from the oral phase? The dance done by mothers and sons is an elaborate one. Mom makes a suggestion. Son does the opposite. Mom decides to do herself what she has asked son to do. Son undermines what mom has done. And so it goes for a thoroughly unpleasant sixteen months until graduation.

Fear is the real reason for college-search procrastination, male or female. For a teen who has never experienced life away from home and has never been subjected to a comprehensive evaluation, the college search is a uniquely terrifying prospect. Few young people have developed the tools they need to deal with it. They are forced to do so as the process moves forward, but in the meantime their first response is to dig in their heels and deny. Seeing this, a parent's natural reaction is to push harder, much to the irritation of the student, who pushes back. Once set in motion, the pattern is hard to break. Here are some suggestions to help parents cope:

- **Bite your tongue.** Parents are always a step ahead of their kids on the college search. Don't fret when it doesn't move on your timetable. Make suggestions, ask questions, and drop reminders, but be prepared for a hasty retreat if you encounter resistance. Many eleventh graders have a hard time getting into the process. Everything will eventually work out.

- **Let others deliver the message.** Parents may not realize it, but they get dumber every year as their kids get older. By a kid's sixteenth birthday, parents are ignorant of any remotely useful information. Make an appointment with the school counselor and talk to him or her about the messages that you think should be conveyed. Then sit back and let someone else be the messenger.

- **Get them on a campus.** There is nothing like visiting a campus to make the process real. Students often find new motivation when they see all the incredible resources that will be at their disposal. If they sit in on an admission presentation, they suddenly realize the competition they'll be up against. For a first visit, almost any plausible college will do. Each visit to a college campus provides a basis for comparison on future visits.

Procrastination is the toughest nut for parents to crack. For advice on advanced cases, see page 119.

> My most productive college visits were the ones without my parents, where I actually stayed in a student's dorm or apartment, went out with them and their friends at night, and had them show me around the campus.
>
> —**University of Southern California student**

Early March is when many high schools begin course sign-ups for the following year. Students always face dilemmas. Do I bail out of Spanish V in order to take a third AP course? Should I continue with art or take a computer course? Do I really need to take calculus? And the bottom line: What will look good to the colleges?

> **I see too many students spend four years establishing a fabulous GPA and activities résumé, then spend too little time on their applications.**
>
> **— Counselor's heads-up**

The answer to the last one is simple. Highly selective colleges want to see top grades in the school's most challenging courses. Just because a student is interested in history doesn't mean colleges will give a free pass on math and science. A key element of every student's application is the high school counselor's rating of his or her curriculum. Most demanding available? Very demanding? Average? At Ivy-type schools, any rating that is not "most demanding" means that you had better be a star athlete or French horn prodigy.

There are always legitimate choices to make. For a student passionate about the life sciences, dropping Spanish V to pick up AP Environmental Science makes perfect sense. In electives like art and computer, a student's interests trump any thought of what might "look good."

In recent years, there has been a backlash against the mindless race to pile on AP courses. A few elite private schools have dumped the AP curriculum in favor of homegrown electives that cater to the interests of students and faculty. Colleges such as University of Chicago have gone on record saying they prefer students who have made intelligent choices in their course selection rather than simply accumulating every conceivable advanced course. (For more on the AP program, see page 76.)

In today's climate of hyper-anxiety, parents must help their kids make sane choices. Mental health is important, too. Happy and productive students are the ones most likely to excel in all phases of twelfth grade—including the college admission game.

MARCH 5–11, 2006

A peek into next week shows that March 15 is the deadline for students to register to take AP exams in May. If you are currently enrolled in an AP course, your school will probably register you automatically to take the exam. The fee is about $82 with limited financial assistance available that may vary from school to school. Check with the school's AP coordinator. About 60 percent of schools nationwide offer AP courses. If you want to take an AP exam but attend one of the 40 percent of schools that do not offer AP, or if you are homeschooled, now is the time to contact a school in your area that does offer them. Students considering this option should head to www.collegeboard.com for an overview of the tests or buy a prep book among the many that are available in bookstores. AP courses are generally a year long, so covering all the material will take some doing.

All-around academic and athletic excellence is the standard for the **Scholar Athlete Milk Mustache of the Year** award, which echoes the popular advertising campaign with the same theme. Twenty-five one-time scholarships of $7,500 are awarded. This week marks the application deadline for one of the nation's premier summer programs for students interested in the arts. Programs at the **Tisch School of New York University** include acting, dramatic writing, musical theater, and film.

Sunday, March 5

☐ Scholar Athlete Milk Mustache of the Year
  (SAMMY) Award. www.whymilk.com

_____

Monday, March 6

_____

_____

Tuesday, March 7

_____   _____

_____   _____

Wednesday, March 8

☐ April SAT, late-registration deadline   _____

_____   _____

Thursday, March 9

_____   _____

_____   _____

Friday, March 10

☐ Tisch Summer High School Programs,   _____
   application deadline.
   www.nyu.edu   _____

Saturday, March 11

_____   _____

_____   _____

Good-bye, 1600. With the advent of the new SAT, the supreme symbol of standardized testing brainpower is now 2400.

So long, SAT Verbal. Students now do battle with two new sections: critical reading and writing. Mere oval-blackening is out, replaced by a twenty-five-minute essay.

These are the most notable features of the new SAT. Despite the new essay requirement and lengthening the test by forty-five minutes (to three hours and forty-five minutes), the news is not all bad. The much-feared analogy section has been scrapped, and so has the bane of the math section: quantitative comparisons.

Although the SAT has undergone nearly a dozen overhauls in its seventy-seven-year history, this one may be the most significant. The College Board always claimed that the test measures all-around reasoning ability rather than achievement in particular courses. But a growing chorus of critics accused the test of being too disconnected from what students learn in school. The analogy section was a particularly notable example: When was the last time an English class sat down to ponder those mind-benders?

According to the Board, the new SAT is a better reflection of what should be learned in a typical high school curriculum. Here is a breakdown of what to expect:

- **Critical Reading.** This is the new name for the old Verbal section. The familiar reading comprehension passages of approximately 400–850 words are still there. To replace the analogies, College Board has added a batch of shorter reading passages of about one hundred to two hundred words.

- **Writing.** This new section includes questions similar to those on the old SAT II: Writing Test. The multiple-choice questions ask students to identify grammar

---

Don't visit more than two colleges in a day. You get bored and tired and college number three won't get a fair chance.

— University of Delaware student

and usage errors and improve the wording of sentences and paragraphs. The essay asks students to state an opinion on a general topic and back it up with evidence taken from their reading and experiences.

• **Math.** The old SAT stopped with algebra and geometry. The new version includes topics often covered in algebra II, from absolute value to quadratic functions. The test also features more challenging geometry, including questions where trigonometry can be used as an alternate method to find the answer. A touch of probability and statistics is also included.

Everyone who is stressed about the new SAT can console themselves with the knowledge that some of the mystery surrounding the test has been dispelled. The SAT is not a yardstick of intelligence, reasoning ability, or anything similar. The College Board says it is a better measure of past and future performance in school. We can all hope that a more straightforward and reliable test will be the ultimate result. Students taking the test in March should consider doing so a second time in May, with June devoted to the SAT Subject Tests.

> At larger schools, I felt like a walking version of my SAT score.
>
> —**Southwestern University student**

MARCH 12–18, 2005

The week's admission deadlines include **Clarkson University, University of Minnesota at Morris, Ripon College,** and **Wittenberg University**. (For a complete list, see Appendix B.) With spring break around the corner, now is the time to follow through on making arrangements for college visits.

   U.S.A. Funds offers one-time scholarships up to $1,500 to minority students with financial need. The **Horace Mann Scholarship** offers twenty-six one-time scholarships of up to $10,000 for children of teachers and other school employees. The **National Federation of Independent Business** offers more than 300 scholarships of up to $10,000 through its Free Enterprise Scholars Program to students who have demonstrated entrepreneurial spirit. Clark's **Summer Science Program** is three weeks and free for the taking for students who have completed eleventh grade. Among the nation's most unique summer programs is the **Freeman Asian Cultural Experience** in Sewanee, which offers participants a free two-week program for students who have completed tenth or eleventh grade. (See Summer for Free, page 90.)

Sunday, March 12

_____

_____

_____

Monday, March 13

_____

_____

_____

Tuesday, March 14

_____

_____

_____

Wednesday, March 15

- ☐ Application deadlines at moderately selective colleges
- ☐ AP Exam registration deadline for homeschooled students and those attending schools not offering AP
- ☐ U.S.A Funds Access to Education Scholarship. www.usafunds.org
- ☐ Horace Mann Scholarship. www.horacemann.com
- ☐ NFIB Free Enterprise Scholarship. www.nfib.com
- ☐ Clark University—Summer Science Program Deadline. www.clarku.edu
- ☐ FACES Asian Studies Summer Program Deadline. www.sewanee.edu

Thursday, March 16

Friday, March 17

- ☐ April ACT, late-registration deadline

Saturday, March 18

MARCH 19–25, 2006

With a late-March lull in the calendar, it makes sense for the Class of 2007 to look toward the crucial standardized tests of April, May, and June. Many students who took the March SAT will want a second shot at the test in May. Others may choose to wait until June 3—especially if they will have extra time to prepare because school is out—but June is also the traditional time for juniors to take the SAT Subject Tests.

Highly selective private colleges, and a few public institutions such as the **University of California**, require the Subject Tests. Before the advent of the new SAT and its writing section, such colleges almost universally required three Subject Tests, but now that the SAT includes Writing, most colleges have reduced their requirement to two tests. A representative sample of these includes **Amherst, Brown, Boston University, Connecticut College, Middlebury, NYU, Pomona, Rice**, and the **UC system**. The handful of hold-outs that still require three include **Harvard, Princeton, Yale, MIT**, and **Georgetown**. Students may take up to three Subject Tests on a single test date and cannot take them on the same date as an SAT. June is generally the recommended date because many students will have just finished a year of studying the subjects. For a complete list of all the schools that require Subject Tests, see Appendix A.

A few of the hundreds of colleges that do not require or recommend SAT Subject Tests are **Colby, University of Denver, George Washington, Gettysburg, Kalamazoo, Marquette**, and **Rhodes**. For most students looking at moderately selective schools, there is no reason to worry about the Subject Tests. However, homeschooled applicants and those from so-so high schools may want to consider the Subject Tests, even when their colleges do not require them, as a way to enhance their credentials.

Sunday, March 19

_____

_____

_____

Monday, March 20

_____

_____

_____

Tuesday, March 21

_____   _____

_____   _____

Wednesday, March 22

_____   _____

_____   _____

Thursday, March 23

_____   _____

_____   _____

Friday, March 24

_____   _____

_____   _____

Saturday, March 25

_____   _____

_____   _____

MARCH 26–31, 2006

The **Young American Creative Patriotic Art** award features three one-time scholarships of $10,000 and is available to students in grades 9–12. One of the most popular universities north of the border, **University of British Columbia**, has its application deadline this week.

Looking ahead to summer, **Landmark Volunteers** offers dozens of community service programs throughout the nation. The program is available to students who have completed grades 9–11 and costs $875 in the form of a tax-deductible contribution.

Sunday, March 26

Monday, March 27

Tuesday, March 28

Wednesday, March 29

☐ **Young American Creative Patriotic Art Award.**
www.ladiesauxvfw.com

_____

_____

Thursday, March 30

_____   _____

_____   _____

Friday, March 31

☐ **University of British Columbia, admission deadline**

☐ **Landmark Volunteers Deposit Deadline.**
www.volunteers.com

_____

_____

SAT AND ACT: WHAT'S THE DIFFERENCE?

Ask someone from Massachusetts about the ACT and you may get blank stare. The same goes if you ask about the SAT in Iowa. The world of college admission is divided into two fiefdoms of

> The most common mistake students make on the essay is to write as if they were doing an English paper—they do not allow their voices to be heard. — Counselor's heads-up

roughly the same size. The SAT was created by a group of Ivy Leaguers and has historically been a sorting mechanism for elite East Coast institutions and their followers. The SAT is also the dominant test on the West Coast. The ACT came out of the University of Iowa and has historically served the Midwest and Mountain West.

The ACT includes sections scored from 1–36 in English, math, reading, and science reasoning.

Like the SAT, the ACT has added an essay section that is 30 minutes long. But unlike the SAT writing section, the ACT essay writing section is optional. (Consult your colleges to see if they require the essay.) The national average for the ACT is between 20 and 21, while the average on the SAT is about 500 on each of the writing, critical reading, and math sections.

The vast majority of colleges will accept either the SAT or ACT to satisfy their core testing requirements. Some highly selective institutions, especially technically oriented places, prefer the SAT because it makes finer distinctions on the high end of the testing range. Any student for whom standardized testing is a strong point should seriously consider taking the SAT.

Though used interchangeably, the tests differ in important ways. The SAT has historically been a test of "reasoning" that emphasizes vocabulary, reading comprehension, and logic. It makes heavy use of "distracters," especially in the math section, which are wrong answers made to look like correct ones. Confident, aggressive problem-solvers who know when people are trying to trick them will do best on the SAT. Relative to the SAT, the ACT is a more straightforward measure of achievement. Students who work hard in school—as opposed to those who are intuitive geniuses—tend to do well on it.

The coming of the new SAT has narrowed the gap between the two tests. The multiple-choice questions on the SAT Writing section resemble those in the ACT's English section, and the SAT's new Math section includes advanced material that aligns it more closely with the ACT Math. Although the new SAT is more like the ACT than the old one was, the tests do retain their distinct personalities.

The tests are similar in two additional ways: Both put students under time pressure and both are grueling marathons.

> **We set deadlines for completion of applications tied to other events, like you can't go skiing at Christmas unless the applications are done by Thanksgiving.**
>
> **—Skidmore College mom**

Most college counselors have had the unpleasant task of sitting down with a B+ student who wants to apply to Harvard, Yale, and Princeton with Penn as the backup school. Since unrealistic expectations tend to run in families, Mom and Dad are often in on the delusion. Part of the problem is that selective colleges are vastly more competitive for admission than they were a generation ago. But the importance of a reality check is crucial, especially at the beginning before anyone's heart gets set on pie in the sky.

Sitting down with the college counselor is a good first step. Often, counselors keep records of how applicants from the school have fared in the past. If the last eight students who have applied to a particular school with your grades and test scores have been denied, that's a clue of what is coming. Counselors are in the business of being professional pessimists when it comes to highly selective schools, and with good reason. They've seen a lot of dreams get dashed. Some are guilty of lowballing a student's prospects on occasion, so don't get discouraged if you think the counselor is selling your chances short.

Another tool in assessing admission chances is the college's profile, which lists ranges for grades and test scores. If a college accepts a third of its applicants or less, a student must have credentials significantly above average (or a special talent) in order to have an even chance of getting in. If a college accepts more than half, students who match the academic profile are likely to get in.

Ambitious applicants should hedge their bets. Most applicants have no trouble identifying dream schools, which are often highly selective. It is also a good idea to include several colleges where the odds are close to 50/50, and then at least two where the odds of admission are likely. Most importantly, every school on the list should be a good match for the student's needs and interests.

MARCH 2006

Avoid "ego-booster" applications. Our daughter told us that she wanted to apply to one of the top schools just to see if she could get in. We reminded her that if she was not serious about these places, there was no point in wasting the time and money.

—University of Illinois and Urbana-Champaign dad

APRIL 2006

LET'S HOPE THAT APRIL will not be the cruelest month for the Class of 2006. Most highly selective institutions will post their decisions on the Internet by April 1 with letters following early in the week of April 3. Wait-listed students should follow up promptly and vigorously. Financial aid applicants who get lowball awards from their top choice college may appeal—preferably using a second, higher award as leverage. (See page 208.) Students wishing to take a year off before college should contact the colleges by phone and follow up with a letter. Students should reply to all offers of admission—including those they choose not to accept—by May 1.

Eleventh graders should continue researching colleges with a goal of finding ten to twelve likely options by the end of school. Families should firm up summer plans and schedule college visits.

WHAT TO DO:

✓ **Saturday, April 1**
Decisions at the most selective colleges mailed and available on the Web

✓ **Monday, April 3**
May SAT and Subject Tests, registration deadline

✓ **Saturday, April 8**
ACT administered

✓ **Friday, April 28**
June SAT and Subject Tests, registration deadline

APRIL 1–8, 2006

Twelfth graders can expect decision letters from the last of their colleges this week and will have until May 1 to respond.

As the Class of 2006 mulls its options, the Class of 2007 should gather a few lessons for next year. Eleventh graders can learn a lot by watching their older friends deal with the final stages of the college search. For instance, there is probably at least one student in the Class of 2006 who applied to, say, twelve colleges. That person was probably admitted at eight schools, more or less, and now has the impossible task of trying to choose one from an unwieldy list of colleges. Lesson: It does not make sense to apply to more than six or eight colleges.

There are other scenarios to watch for. Did anybody in the Class of 2006 aim too high and get turned down at every school except for an undesired safety? Did anybody come to grief because their parents decided at the last minute that they could not afford Dream U? Look for pitfalls to avoid, and get pointers from the students whose college search turned out right.

The **Yoshiyama Award**, based solely on community service, requires a nomination and nets winners a one-time award of $5,000. One of the nation's biggest providers of scholarships for minority students, the **Jackie Robinson Foundation**, offers scholarships of up to $24,000 over four years for students with outstanding credentials who exceed 900 on the Critical Reading and Math portions of the SAT or 21 on the ACT. CMU's **Summer Programs for Diversity** are free, six-week programs for rising eleventh and twelfth graders in math and science and fine arts.

Saturday, April 1

- ☐ Decisions at highly selective colleges mailed and available on the Web
- ☐ Yoshiyama Award. www.hitachifoundation.org/yoshiyama
- ☐ Jackie Robinson Foundation Scholarship. www.jackierobinson.org
- ☐ University of Arizona, Gustavus Adolphus College, Howard University and University of Iowa, admission deadline
- ☐ Carnegie Mellon University—Summer Programs for Diversity. www.cmu.edu

Sunday, April 2

_____

_____

Monday, April 3

☐ May SAT and Subject Tests, registration deadline

_____

Tuesday, April 4

_____

_____

Wednesday, April 5

_____

_____

Thursday, April 6

_____

_____

_____

_____

Friday, April 7

_____

_____

_____

_____

Saturday, April 8

☐ ACT administered

_____

_____

_____

APRIL 9–15, 2006

Mid-April offers the newly admitted a chance for a triumphant victory tour. Most colleges host roll-out-the-red-carpet days for accepted students at about this time, and it makes sense to do one last visit if there is any uncertainty about where to go. Such programs allow students to see the campus once again—with the eight-hundred-pound monkey of admission off their backs—and students also get to rub shoulders with their future classmates. Considering the amount of money that you will be forking over for tuition, the expense of one more trip is a small price to pay.

Eleventh graders planning summer college visits should set their itinerary and call now for the best chance of getting an interview. (See page 84.)

The **AMVETS scholarship** offers ten awards totaling $4,000 each to veterans and their dependents. Wabash's **Opportunities to Learn about Business** is a free weeklong program for rising twelfth graders. (See Summer for Free, page 90.)

Sunday, April 9

_____   _____

_____   _____

_____   _____

Monday, April 10

_____   _____

_____   _____

_____   _____

Tuesday, April 11

Wednesday, April 12

Thursday, April 13

Friday, April 14

Saturday, April 15

☐ AMVETS National Scholarship. www.amvets.org

☐ Wabash College—Opportunities to Learn about Business Summer Program. www.wabash.edu/olab

The National Youth Leadership Forum is the most prominent organization on the college prep scene that did not exist in 1990. Every year, thousands of students are plied with invitations to attend its programs to the tune of more than $1,000 per week plus transportation expenses. Are these programs worth it? Students and parents nationwide want to know.

NYLF is a powerhouse of marketing and an interesting study in persuasion. The organization runs dozens of five- and ten-day programs annually, in cities throughout the country, that focus on Medicine, Law, Technology, and Defense/Intelligence/Diplomacy. NYLF builds its mailing list in a variety of ways, but one of the most important is by currying favor with high school teachers. It aggressively seeks "nominations" from them, cagily asking that they provide the names and addresses of students with the admonition that "space in the program is strictly limited." Only students with a 3.3 GPA may be nominated—about half the student body at many schools.

Armed with its nominations, NYLF mails its pitch to the students—not as a money-grubbing solicitor, but to bestow recognition on students who are starved for positive feedback and résumé builders. In reality, NYLF on the résumé means about as much as Who's Who among American High School Students (in other words, not much). A small fraction of attendees receive financial aid, but every college admission office knows that wealthy families who can pay the bill are the primary constituency.

But what about the programs? From everything we can gather, they are very good. At a recent Forum on Medicine, students heard lectures from leading medical professionals, visited medical schools, and completed a diagnosis simulation like those done by medical students. A recent Forum on Technology allowed students to meet with executives from Dell and IBM, among others.

Students generally enjoy the NYLF experience—especially the opportunity to make new friends who share their interests. It is NYLF's methods of persuasion rather than its programs that make many educators and us uncomfortable. Attending an NYLF program is not a meaningful honor, but it may be worthwhile depending on the student's interests and the family budget.

ADMISSION 101: THE BIG PICTURE

Many students (and parents) never get beyond the idea that college admission is a cold calculation of grades and test scores. They picture faceless committees passing judgment with ruthless efficiency on the hapless souls with the audacity to send in an application.

> Way too many colleges say that they don't emphasize SAT or ACT scores in the admission process.
>
> —Counselor's heads-up

Grades and scores are important, just as experience and references are important in getting a job. No one can get into college—or get a job—if they're not qualified. But qualifications only take you so far. The clincher is often the human element—the ability to interact, to make oneself vulnerable, and to have a conversation with admission officers across the chasm of a process that, because of its scale, does risk being impersonal.

Picture a college admission officer. Did he or she get into this job to be a standardized test bean counter? A transcript analysis technician? Are admission officers in it for the money? Strange as it may seem, most admission people stay in their jobs because they like working with teenagers. They want and even crave contact with applicants. Though buffeted by administrative pressures, they cherish the notion that they can make a difference.

Students must never lose sight of the real people that orchestrate the process. Call, write, email, interview—anything to keep a real conversation going without obvious brown-nosing or attention-getting stunts. It isn't easy, but students with the moxie to put themselves on the line are generally rewarded.

> Make sure that your tour guide is realistic. There is no school that only has good characteristics. Search for the flaws.
>
> —College of Charleston student

Building a manageable list of college options—say, ten to twelve colleges—is one of the most important tasks in spring of eleventh grade. Here is a list of ways to do it.

- **Read the One-Hour College Finder in the _Fiske Guide to Getting into the Right College_**. You'll find thumbnail sketches, organized by category, of several hundred of the nation's top colleges. For comprehensive descriptions, consult the _Fiske Guide to Colleges_.

- **Run an Internet search.** The Web is great for generating lists of colleges with particular criteria. You can sort by size, location, major, and dozens more traits. Our choice among the many sites is www.collegeboard.com.

- **Poll friends, teachers, and relatives.** Suggest that your son or daughter talk to students in grade twelve who share their interests. Contact friends currently in college when they come home for summer vacation.

- **Talk to some experts.** We've said it before—if you have a career interest, try to find a contact in the field. When planning a college visit, make an appointment with someone in a department or field you are considering. Most faculty will give you honest advice even if it doesn't steer you to their school.

- **Read college catalogues and viewbooks.** Most of this material falls under the heading of glitzy advertising, so look for the substance rather than the sizzle, such as course offerings, majors, and distribution requirements.

- **Talk to your counselor.** At schools with strong college counseling, this approach may be best of all. School counselors have the advantage of knowing you and knowing the colleges. Nine times out of ten, their advice is worth heeding.

Today's generation of students would rather log on than grab a pen and paper. It is now possible to point and click your way to college—at least of most of the way. Here are some ways that the Internet comes in handy:

- **Electronic test registration.** College Board (www.collegeboard.com) and ACT (www.act.org) are going all out to encourage families to register for the SAT and ACT online. Confirmation of registration is immediate and there is an email reminder before the test day for anyone with very early Alzheimer's.

- **Searching for colleges.** Websites ranging from College Board to Princeton Review (www.princetonreview. com) and *U.S.News & World Report* (www.usnews.com) have search features that allow students to make choices in dozens of categories such as size, location, intended major, selectivity, and student life. With just a few clicks, students can generate a list of schools that share the qualities they seek.

- **Financial aid estimation and scholarships.** Head to www.collegeboard.com or www.finaid.org and click on "financial aid estimation." Within fifteen minutes, families can get an estimate of how much they will be expected to pay for college. For the Web's best free scholarship search site, head to www.fastweb.com.

- **College websites.** You'll find virtually everything at the college's website that you would find in its publications—and then some. A hint: Instead of going directly to the college's official website, do a category search in Yahoo! or your favorite search engine. You'll learn loads of interesting tidbits from student-produced sites, such as the online version of the campus newspaper.

Filing applications online is another popular use of the Web. (See page 134.) One thing you can't find on the Web is a place for candid, authoritative evaluations of the nation's best colleges. For that, you'll need to find a copy of another volume in the Fiske series, the *Fiske Guide to Colleges*.

APRIL 16–22, 2006

By now, most students in the Class of 2006 will have figured out where they are going next year. If that includes you, don't procrastinate about sending in your acceptance of the offer with a deposit (and sending a brief Dear John letter to the other schools). Colleges often settle important details like housing on a first-come, first-served basis. If you are given a choice of dorms and don't have a clue, contact a current student who graduated from your high school, or simply call the admission office and ask to speak to one. All dorms are not created equal.

A glance into next week reveals that April 28 is the deadline for eleventh graders to register for the June SAT. For those in the Class of 2007 aiming at highly selective colleges, most counselors recommend this date for the SAT Subject tests. Those looking at schools that don't require the Subject Tests may want to think about taking another SAT, or consider taking the ACT on June 10 (deadline May 5). Our recommendation to consider the ACT is particularly strong for those who were disappointed with their SAT scores and may do better on the ACT.

Sunday, April 16

Monday, April 17

Tuesday, April 18

_____

_____

_____

Wednesday, April 19

_____

_____

_____

Thursday, April 20

_____

_____

_____

_____

_____

_____

Friday, April 21

_____

_____

_____

_____

_____

_____

Saturday, April 22

_____

_____

_____

_____

_____

_____

April 23–30, 2006

For the Class of 2006, a few last-minute scholarship opportunities remain. The **Ayn Rand Essay Contest**, sponsored by the foundation that carries on the work of the famed novelist/philosopher, offers sixteen one-time awards between $1,000 and $10,000 for essays on *The Fountainhead*. The contest is open to eleventh and twelfth graders. The **Tylenol Scholarship** is one of the largest in the country, offering ten one-time awards of $10,000 and 150 scholarships of $1,000 to students who plan to major in health-related fields. The **Holocaust Remembrance Project Essay Contest**, open to students in grades 9–12, makes ten one-time awards of $5,000 along with smaller cash prizes. Boston University's **Summer Institute for Television, Film, and Radio Production** is popular and selective. It is open to high school students between ages fourteen and eighteen.

Sunday, April 23

Monday, April 24

Tuesday, April 25

☐ Ayn Rand Essay Contest.
www.aynrand.org/contests

Wednesday, April 26

Thursday, April 27

Friday, April 28

☐ June SAT and Subject Tests, registration deadline

Saturday, April 29

Sunday, April 30

☐ The Tylenol Scholarship.
www.scholarship.tylenol.com

☐ Holocaust Remembrance Project Essay Contest.
www.holocaust.hklaw.com

☐ Boston University Institute for Television, Film, and
Radio Production. www.bu.edu/com/itrp

WHEN MOM AND DAD RUN AMOK: COLLEGE COUNSELORS TELL ALL

You know they mean well, but sometimes parents do the dumbest things. High school counselors see more than their share of these bloopers and missteps. We asked the Fiske College Counselors Advisory Group, listed on page 247, to discuss the common parental mistakes. Here are a few excerpts:

- "I had a parent who called the admission office of a particular college on a weekly basis. In the end, the admission rep called me to say that they were not taking the student because the father had been such a pest. He had even told them that he was retiring at the end of the school year and that the family planned to move near the college and he wanted to volunteer in the admission office!"

- "In my opinion, one of the biggest mistakes parents make is looking only at 'name brand' schools as possibilities for their children. There are so many fantastic colleges out there, yet many, if not most, go virtually unnoticed because parents and students alike get stuck on the rankings they read about in major magazines such as *U.S. News*."

- "Parents make the mistake of opening the student's mail. This is a big no-no. Students are not accustomed to getting mail, and then suddenly in tenth and eleventh grade, they feel important! One of my parents was so eager to read the outcome for her son's college application that she proceeded to steam it open over the tea kettle. She never expected that the letter would actually catch on fire! So she had to put the burnt letter on the table with a Post-it note—confessing this act to her son."

> **Start early because students have so much to deal with their senior year that they are sometimes overwhelmed.**
>
> **—University of San Diego mom**

- "Families need to understand the role of the counselor. They make the mistake of thinking that the counselor's job is to get their child into their top-choice colleges, no matter how unreasonable that choice may be. They seem to think that we can persuade Harvard to take a B student because we have a buddy-buddy relationship with Bill Fitzsimmons. Sometimes our relationships can work with borderline students, but colleges want students who will succeed at their schools."

> Very few parents understand how the admission process has changed in the last decade. Colleges that they think are backups simply aren't.
>
> —Counselor's heads-up

- "The one piece of advice I give most regularly is to back off. When a parent pushes too early, or expresses a strong preference for one of the colleges a student is choosing between, the student usually balks and the result is the opposite of what the parent intended. Our charges are at the brink of adulthood and make their own choices. They are programmed to struggle for their independence, and wise parents respect that and guide them only with the lightest of touches."

- "I had a senior who was accepted to her first-love school—Georgetown. She was also accepted to Texas A&M with a full-ride scholarship. Her parents took her to Georgetown several times for visits and programs and encouraged her and were excited with her through the entire application process. In April, they decided they did not want her to go that far from home and insisted she accept A&M's offer. She was devastated but did what her parents asked. After seeing their daughter's spirit and enthusiasm leave her, they relented (on May 2) and said she could go to Georgetown. I think realizing that their daughter would actually give up her dream to please them opened their eyes to what they were doing."

A Pitch for Small Colleges

Their names don't necessarily set hearts aflutter. Places like College of Wooster, Whitman, or Guilford—to name three—are beneath the radar screen of the cocktail-party circuit. They're among the dozens of small liberal arts colleges enrolling roughly one thousand to three thousand students that dot the national landscape. Small colleges are out of favor in today's college admission game. Everybody wants to go where the action is—to do the internship scene in Washington, join the cast of thousands in Berkeley, or rub shoulders with the bohemians in Greenwich Village. With some exceptions, small colleges tend to be in out-of-the-way places, and a disproportionate number of good ones are in the Midwest, far from the nation's glamor spots.

We don't deny that large institutions in exciting cities are the right choice for many students. We simply think it is unfortunate that so many students won't even consider small colleges. A few of their advantages include:

- **Quality teaching.** Small colleges nearly always provide more access to faculty than big ones. And with only undergraduates on campus, students have a better shot at research opportunities.

- **A well-rounded life.** Any student who loves being involved in many different activities should consider a small college, where the student government, the newspaper, and other organizations are more accessible to the typical student.

- **A place to belong.** Studies consistently show that students do better academically when they are involved in the life of their community. Being a face in the crowd often appeals to students who have overdosed on high school, but, in the end, the reality of anonymity may not be so wonderful.

The issue of large versus small is an important one for many students, and there are additional plusses and minuses on both sides. A more thorough weighing of this issue can be found in the *Fiske Guide to Getting into the Right College.*

THE LONG AND WINDING ROAD TO AN ATHLETIC SCHOLARSHIP

From the time they were knee-high, many high school students have fantasized about playing sports in college and beyond. To make the dream a reality takes persistence, nerve, major athletic talent—and an early start on the college selection process. By spring of eleventh grade, aspiring athletes should be contacting coaches and expressing interest. But before we offer advice to athletic hopefuls, a discussion of the pitfalls of college sports are in order. Most importantly:

- **Playing in college is a huge commitment.** Even at the Division III level, the necessary effort dwarfs what it takes in high school. Long hours of practice and in-season road trips sap energy that would otherwise be available for schoolwork.

- **Getting a spot is harder than it used to be.** The days are over when better-than-average high school athletes could walk on. Today's generation of students is primed to compete for scholarships, or to get the admission advantage that comes from being a Division III recruited athlete.

- **Be prepared to apply early.** Many coaches pressure applicants to apply ED or EA. They say, in not so many words, that if you don't apply early, they can't help you. Be ready to file your application as early as September of twelfth grade, and think ahead about how you will react when a coach starts leaning on you. Don't be buffaloed into a commitment if better choices are out there.

- **Coaches can be sleazebags.** There—we said it. Many coaches have integrity, but others play a shell game. The drill: Recruit five students for one spot on the team, then dump the four also-rans when the real first choice signs on the dotted line.

> Don't apply to eighteen colleges like I did! Either narrow down your choices or start saving now for application fees.
>
> —University of Texas at Austin student

APRIL 2006

Some students assume that Division III schools are less concerned about athletics than those in Division I or II, but that is not always the case. Although they don't give scholarships, elite small colleges have the highest percentage of students who are recruited athletes. These colleges may not play on national TV, but colleges assume that a victory over Archrival U makes the old grads happy and can mean big bucks in donations.

The first step in becoming a recruited athlete is to talk to the high school or club coach. Students should ask for an honest evaluation and get suggestions for colleges where they might fit in. The next step is to crank out letters—lots of them—to express interest. Pertinent information may include club tournaments or summer camps where the student will be playing. A one-page sports résumé should generally go along with the letter, and with some sports, families should make a video showing skill drills or game highlights. If the high school or club coach volunteers to contact a college coach, so much the better.

A few athletes won't have to bother with any of this. They are the superstars all the coaches want. The vast majority of aspiring athletes might be good enough, could be good enough, and must hustle for everything they get.

> Admission officers at highly selective colleges are too enthusiastic during interviews. Students leave those meetings encouraged to apply, even if they stand no chance of getting in.
>
> —Counselor's heads-up

MAY–JUNE 2006

IF YOU'VE EVER WONDERED WHAT drinking from a fire hose is like, try taking three AP tests in a two-week span. Both juniors and seniors will have the pleasure of this experience beginning May 1. Wait-listed seniors should continue to follow up with these colleges. Families should watch for mailings from First Choice U, especially with regard to housing and course registration. Families should make plans to attend summer orientation programs where applicable.

After APs are over, the Class of 2007 should turn its attention to the SAT Subject Tests in June. They should also consider taking the June ACT.

WHAT TO DO:

✓ **Friday, May 5**
June ACT, registration deadline

✓ **Saturday, May 6**
SAT and Subject Tests administered

✓ **May 1–12**
AP exams

✓ **Saturday, June 3**
SAT and Subject Tests administered

✓ **Saturday, June 10**
ACT administered

MAY 1–6, 2006

May 1 is the day of decision for Class of 2006, and it is a deadline not to be trifled with. Applicants who procrastinate past this day without sending a deposit to their college of choice risk losing their place in the class. When more students accept a college's offer of admission than it expects, the threat is real. Families should also understand that sending deposits to two institutions is considered dirty pool. By doing so, they're keeping a hapless wait-listed student in limbo while they take their sweet time in deciding where to go. AP exams begin this week, with morning exams starting at 8:00 a.m. and afternoon exams beginning at noon.

Institutions with May 1 application deadlines include **Clemson, Texas Tech**, and **University of Utah**. The **Jane Austen Society** offers a prize of $1,000 for first place in its essay contest, open to students in grades 9–12. The June ACT, with its registration deadline this week, is the last standardized test administered before next fall.

Monday, May 1

☐ Candidate's reply date, Class of 2006

☐ Application deadlines at moderately selective colleges

☐ Jane Austen Society Essay Contest. www.jasna.org

☐ AP English Language Exam (morning)

☐ AP French Language Exam, AP Human Geography Exam (afternoon)

Tuesday, May 2

☐ AP Computer Science A Exam, Computer Science B Exam, AP Spanish Language Exam (morning)

☐ AP Statistics Exam (afternoon)

Wednesday, May 3

☐ AP Calculus AB Exam, AP Calculus BC Exam, AP Music Theory Exam (morning)

☐ AP World History Exam (afternoon)

Thursday, May 4

☐ AP English Literature Exam (morning)

☐ AP French Literature Exam, AP German Language Exam (afternoon)

Friday, May 5

☐ June ACT, registration deadline
☐ AP U.S. History Exam (morning)

☐ AP European History Exam, AP Studio Art Portfolios due (afternoon)

Saturday, May 6

☐ SAT and Subject Tests administered

MAY 7–13, 2006

AP exam week is the final reckoning for students who have spent an entire year reading, writing, and cramming. In many schools, students can take the morning off from school prior to an afternoon AP, or afternoon off for an exam the next morning. Scores usually arrive in the mail at school in early July, though students can call and get their scores by phone beginning July 1 for the incredibly low price of only $15. The upside of surviving APs is that the final few weeks of school are usually a piece of cake.

The **University of Dallas** has the distinction of sponsoring one of the earliest institutional scholarship deadlines we know of. Juniors who attend an open house program on the U of D campus in either February or April are invited to apply for the **Aspiring Scholars Award** by a May 10 deadline for renewable scholarships of up to $8,000.

Sunday, May 7

_____   _____

_____   _____

_____   _____

Monday, May 8

☐ AP Biology Exam, AP Italian Language Exam (morning)

☐ AP Physics B and C Exams (afternoon)

_____   _____

_____   _____

Tuesday, May 9

☐ AP U.S. Government and Politics Exam (morning)

_____

_____

☐ AP Comparative Government and Politics Exam (afternoon)

_____

Wednesday, May 10

☐ June SAT and Subject Tests, late-registration deadline
☐ AP Chemistry Exam, AP Environmental Science Exam (morning)

☐ AP Psychology Exam (afternoon)
☐ University of Dallas Aspiring Scholars Award Program. www.udallas.edu

Thursday, May 11

☐ AP Macroeconomics Exam, AP Art History Exam (morning)

_____

☐ AP Microeconomics Exam (afternoon)

_____

_____

Friday, May 12

☐ AP Spanish Literature Exam (morning)
☐ AP Latin Literature Exam, AP Latin Vergil Exam (afternoon)

Saturday, May 13

_____

_____

_____

THE APs: A CLOSER LOOK

Over one million students nationwide take AP tests every year, a hefty figure that has grown by leaps and bounds in recent years. AP courses follow a standard curriculum designed to be comparable to an introductory college course. The test is graded on a scale of one to five, with a score of five roughly equal to an A in an introductory college course, a four equal to a B, a three equal to C, and a two equal to a D. Many colleges and universities grant credit for high AP scores, though some have become more stingy with it as the percentage of students with AP courses has risen. With credit no longer a given, AP has morphed from a placement tool to an admission credential that serves as a proxy for the rigor of a student's curriculum.

AP tests are generally divided into two parts: a multiple-choice section and a free-response section that may include essays or problem-solving, depending on the subject.

AP scores can be reported to the colleges in the same way as all the other College Board scores. Each school gets a sticker listing a student's AP scores, which is often put on the back of the transcript. However, if they so choose, students can request that these scores be taken off the transcript and not reported. Students can also report AP scores officially via the College Board for $14, though this may not be necessary if the score is on the transcript.

Unlike the SAT and the Subject Tests, College Board does allow students to officially report some AP scores and not others. Students are often reluctant to submit scores of 1 or 2 for exams taken in tenth or eleventh grade. But herein lies a dilemma: The high school transcript includes the AP course, so not submitting a score lets the colleges know that the score was probably low. For the most part, a score of 2 should be sent. Chalk up a 1 to having a bad day and don't worry about it.

The major competitor to AP, much less prominent in the U.S. but well-known abroad, is the International Baccalaureate (IB) program. IB differs from AP in that it includes the option of a comprehensive, two-year diploma rather than an a la carte menu of courses. For more information on IB, head to www.ibo.org. More on AP is available at www.collegeboard.com.

It is hardly surprising that most high school students have no idea what they want to do when they grow up. The real wonder is that anyone expects them to know. Our secondary education system does a reasonably good job of exposing students to English, math, history, and so on, and a terrible job of exposing them to potential careers. Ideally, classroom study of the liberal arts should be supplemented by consistent exposure to various careers.

> We began by visiting colleges during my son's junior year in high school. If we had a vacation or business trip, we would visit the colleges in that area.
>
> —University of San Diego mom

Parents, a savvy move is to help schedule shadowing experiences to explore career possibilities. If your student has an interest in architecture, see if you can help him or her connect with an architect for a day or a week of observation. If your son or daughter is interested in law, find out if the school counselor knows lawyers in the community who might be helpful. In addition to learning about a career, students learn about the world of work and get a chance to step outside their comfort zone. Spring break can be an ideal time, and many a summer job has developed from a few days of shadowing.

The Internet can also provide some valuable tools for exploring interests. At www.advisorteam.com, students can learn more about their temperament and learning style with a free interactive program. At www.profiler.com, students can take the well-known Campbell Interest and Skills Survey for a fee of $17.95. For resources on particular careers, www.collegeboard.com has a browseable resource area with extensive information.

There is no need to rush career training in the classroom. In college, liberal arts students do just fine in the job market while getting a well-rounded education. No matter what their interests, students can benefit from using extracurricular activities, internships, and shadowing activities to get a head start on finding a career path.

MAY 14–20, 2006

With APs in the rearview mirror, seniors are home free and juniors can breathe a sigh of relief (unless they still have final exams). The Class of 2006 will still find a handful of scholarships in play, notably twenty-five awards from the **Society of Women Engineers** worth up to $5,000 (renewable) and available to males as well as females. The weeklong **Step Up to Leadership** program is free for students who have completed ninth or tenth grades. (See Summer for Free, page 90.)

Sunday, May 14

Monday, May 15

☐ Society of Women Engineers Scholarship.
www.swe.org

☐ Claremont McKenna College—Step Up to
Leadership Summer Program. www.mckenna.edu

Tuesday, May 16

Wednesday, May 17

Thursday, May 18

Friday, May 19

☐ June ACT, late-registration deadline

Saturday, May 20

MAY 21–27, 2006

Late May is the time that students in the Class of 2007 should have a working list of about ten colleges. If you're still considering 20 or more schools, choices must be made. The time is at hand to plan summer and fall visits, and there is no way you'll be able to take a good look at more than about 10–12 colleges. Dust off your college guides, surf the college websites, and narrow it down. One strategy is to combine colleges with similar characteristics and then figure out which ones you want to eliminate. Suppose your list includes roughly the same number of medium-sized universities and small colleges. If the small colleges on the list include **Allegheny, Bucknell, Franklin & Marshall, Gettysburg, Lafayette, Lake Forest**, and **Susquehanna,** consider the group as a whole with the goal of cutting two. **Bucknell, F&M**, and **Lafayette** are the most selective three—which of the three is your least favorite? **Allegheny, Gettysburg**, and **Lake Forest** are also comparable in selectivity. Is there one of these you can cut? By paring your list with an eye toward the big picture, you can ensure that you have a diverse and balanced selection of choices.

Sunday, May 21

_____

_____

Monday, May 22

_____

_____

Tuesday, May 23

_____

_____

_____

_____

Wednesday, May 24

Thursday, May 25

Friday, May 26

Saturday, May 27

MAY 28–31, 2006

With no deadlines as May comes to a close, procrastinators in the Class of 2007 should hustle to line up a worthwhile summer agenda. The deadline for many summer programs will have passed, but many colleges will still take applications if they have space. Work is a perfectly honorable way to spend the summer, but rather than flipping burgers, try to find something related to a possible career interest, even if it means you must volunteer. The best idea of all may be to find a professional to shadow in a field of interest. (See Thinking about Careers, page 77.) For a rising senior in high school, a meaningful experience is more important than a few extra dollars.

Sunday, May 28

_____

_____

Monday, May 29

_____

_____

Tuesday, May 30

_____

_____

Wednesday, May 31

_____

_____

Preparation for the SAT is big business nationwide for outfits such as Kaplan and Princeton Review. Less attention is devoted to prep for the SAT Subject Tests, but the fact is that studying for these tests is likely to pay even bigger dividends.

Unlike the SAT, the Subject Tests cover a relatively limited amount of material. And unlike AP tests, which test a standard curriculum covered in AP courses, SAT Subject Tests do not always seamlessly match the curriculum of high school courses. Consider the Subject Test in U.S. History. Like all the rest, it is 100 percent multiple choice, with questions distributed relatively equally among topics from the American colonies to the present. But many high school courses emphasize some topics more than others, proceed thematically, or don't require coverage of a broad range of facts. Before you take any Subject Test, go online to www.collegeboard.com and take a peek at the sample questions there. If some of the material is outside the scope of your high-school course, your best bet may be to buy a prep book.

As to choosing particular tests, the best approach is usually to stick with sequential courses such as math, science, and foreign language. Math Level II is the most universal choice for any student who gets to pre-calculus or the equivalent by eleventh grade. (Math Level I may be suitable for those in algebra II or the equivalent.) A logical choice in science or language is generally the subject that the student has taken in eleventh grade. To do a foreign language Subject Test, students need to have a minimum of three years of study under their belts, though a fourth or fifth from middle school would be better. Since all but a handful of ultra-elite colleges now require only two SAT Subject Tests, students have greater ability to focus in-depth on each test. (See pages 222 and 223 for the relevant lists.) Some students may want to get both tests out of the way in June; others may want to prepare for one in June and one in October. If the whole Subject Test thing is freaking you out, keep in mind that many schools will let you opt out of

---

Getting my application done during the summer before my senior year was incredibly helpful.

—Colby College student

If procrastination has slowed down the planning for summer college visits, now is the time to firm up the details. The first half of August is the peak interval for visits at the nation's selective colleges—call well in advance for the best shot at an interview. June might be a better time to go if you have the flexibility. The crowds will be smaller, and more faculty and coaches will be in their offices.

> When you visit a college, try to arrange an appointment with a professor who teaches in your area of interest.
>
> **—Valparaiso University student**

The main drawback of a summer visit is that the real students will not be there. The hip-looking Frisbee throwers wearing the backward baseball caps are likely to be high-school-age impostors there for a summer program. A full-time student will probably be your tour guide, though he or she may not stray far from a spiel that the admission office has prepared. Look for unguarded moments of candor.

The key to a successful visit is to help your son or daughter line up as many points of contact as possible. The student should make the call and be as politely pushy as possible. An interview is option number one, unless the student is particularly shy. Admission offices say that interviews can only help you, and they're right. Ninety percent of it is just showing up and getting the brownie points for being interested. An interview helps the admission office put a name with a face—rarely does a student encounter an inquisition-style interviewer, though a few are out there. If the student hits it off with the interviewer, or gets on a roll talking about one of her interests, so much the better.

> Too often, students choose safety schools with a "hope to hell I don't have to go there" attitude.
>
> **—Counselor's heads-up**

If an interview is not in the cards, ask to meet with a faculty member in an area of interest. Some academic departments have designated faculty members who handle this assignment. If this is not possible, option number three is an admission information session conducted by a staff person at the college. Anyone with a special interest—such as athletics or music—should also ask about coaches and directors and try to make appointments with them directly if necessary.

It is asking a lot for a seventeen-year-old to be the point-person in making these arrangements. Parents should be prepared to step in and help when necessary, or to ask the college counselor to do so. Colleges will vary in their responsiveness, and you'll learn a little about how each operates. (For a comprehensive overview of college visits and interviews, see the *Fiske Guide to Getting into the Right College*.)

HIGH SCHOOL COURSES VERSUS THOSE AT A LOCAL COLLEGE

Advanced students seeking a challenge—and a pat on the back for going above and beyond—sometimes wonder whether they might be better off taking courses at a local college rather than their high school's honors or AP courses. In most cases, they won't be. AP culminates in a grade recognized nationwide, and the caliber of student at your local college may not be as high as in an advanced high school course. A college course is generally the better option only if a student is looking at specialized subject matter, such as a language like Russian or Japanese. If the subject is in the high school curriculum, the best bet is to take it there.

> Highly selective colleges are often not forthright about their admission criteria and seek applications from students who have little hope of being admitted. The reason is to keep the deny rate high.
>
> —Counselor's heads-up

JUNE 2006

June marks the last round of SAT testing until October, with most students taking the Subject Tests. On test day, students are allowed to change their minds about which ones they wish to take, though students may not take more tests than they were registered for. The last ACT of the school year is Saturday, June 10.

Chemagination is a national essay contest sponsored by the American Chemical Society with awards determined at the local level. This week's deadline is for the national competition, but interested students must first enter locally. Head to the link below to find your contact. The National Foundation for the Advancement of the Arts sponsors the **Arts Recognition and Talent Search** (ARTS), one of the nation's most prestigious competitions for students in dance, film and video, jazz, music, photography, theater, visual arts, voice, and writing. Hundreds of one-time scholarships up to $25,000 are available. The program is also the gateway to the **Presidential Scholars in the Arts** recognition program. June 1 is an early deadline with a second round on October 1. The **Hispanic Scholarship Fund** and the **Society of Hispanic Professional Engineers** team up to offer one-time awards of up to $2,500 for students with intended majors in math, computer science, and engineering.

Thursday, June 1

☐ Arts Recognition and Talent Search, early deadline. www.artsawards.org

Tuesday, June 6

☐ Chemagination Essay Contest. www.chemistry.org

Saturday, June 3

☐ SAT and Subject Tests administered

Saturday, June 10

☐ ACT administered

Thursday, June 15

☐ Hispanic Scholarship Fund/Society of Hispanic
Professional Engineers Scholarship Program.
www.shpe.org

_____

_____

_____

TOP FIVE PITFALLS TO A SUCCESSFUL COLLEGE VISIT

5. Mom and Dad argue about directions—and the family arrives twenty minutes late.

4. Mom compulsively adjusts son's collar in the waiting room.

3. Dad decides he has a few additional questions after the information session; daughter turns crimson.

2. Mom asks tour guide if the dining hall food has enough roughage.

1. Son pretends he doesn't know Mom for the rest of the tour.

SUMMER 2006

IF YOU'VE FOLLOWED THE ADVICE OF THIS BOOK, you have scheduled a challenging and enjoyable lineup of summer activities. Balance is the key, so try to avoid overload and make sure you get a break from the rigors of school. That said, there are many things students can do in the summer to get a leg up on the hectic grind of twelfth grade. We realize that most of these are a pipedream, but here is the list:

- **Do a draft of a college essay.** Some students are lucky enough to attend schools that help them with essay drafts in eleventh grade. For those who don't, the summer is a great time to do a first draft of an essay. Students can take a peek at the essay topics of colleges they are interested in or write a general essay that could be tailored to various questions. One good strategy is to write the essay, put it aside, and then revisit it in October.
- **Do a résumé or activity chart.** Most applications ask students to write a list of activities, honors, and employment for their application. Doing it now helps avoid omissions and makes it easier to deal with the idiosyncrasies of particular application forms.
- **Prepare for standardized tests.** For students who were disappointed with their spring standardized test scores, the summer is a relaxed time to bone up for the fall administration. A few vocabulary words a night can help increase word power. Now is also a good time to take a coaching course that won't interfere with schoolwork.

- Work on the scholarship search. The admission process is work enough for the fall. Now may be the only sane time to identify possible scholarships. Many applications are downloadable online and can be completed in the summer even though they may not be due for months.

Grinding on college applications is not anyone's idea of a fun summer, and we would never suggest such a thing if not for the juggernaut that will hit in the fall.

SUMMER FOR FREE

Families willing to cough up a few thousand dollars will find myriad summer opportunities. The list that follows is a sampling of the best programs that don't cost a dime. Because they are free, they tend to be competitive and therefore will add more teeth to a student's college résumé than a top-dollar Ivy League summer school.

We also offer a second list of programs that have historically been intended for students from underrepresented minority groups. These programs have recently come under legal attack for excluding white students, and some are now technically open to disadvantaged students from any background. Many colleges offer programs like these; we merely include a sample of the best and most interesting of them.

A third list highlights a few programs that, while not free, are low cost or noteworthy.

Open to All

Claremont McKenna College. Step Up to Leadership Program. Open to rising tenth and eleventh graders nominated by their principals, this weeklong program affiliated with CMC's Kravis Leadership Institute is free but does not include transportation costs. Claremont McKenna is a selective private college in southern California. Deadline: May 15. More information: www.mckenna.edu

Clark University. Summer Science Program. Students who are between the eleventh and twelfth grades can enjoy three free weeks of thematic science study at Clark, a medium-sized university in Worcester, Massachusetts. Deadline: March 15. More information: www.clarku.edu

Congressional Page Program. Students can spend a summer, a semester, or a year delivering messages to members of Congress—and get paid for it. Two four-week sessions for sixty-six students each are available in the summer. Students live in their own residence hall and get paid the equivalent of about $14,500 per year. More information: contact your senator or representative in congress.

> My visits helped me find out about things like class size and the number of teaching assistants, but most helpful was just seeing the attitude of students in class.
>
> —Harvard University student

Governor's School. The programs vary by state, and not all states have a governor's school. The schools vary in length and focus but are typically housed on a university campus. Most are free. For more information, contact your high school counselor or state department of education.

Massachusetts Institute of Technology and California Institute of Technology. Research Science Institute. Founded by Admiral Hyman Rickover, RSI is the nation's premier summer program for aspiring science whiz kids. The program lasts six weeks, and everything except transportation is free. Students who get in here can probably get in anywhere. Deadline: February 1. More information: www.cee.org/rsi

University of the South—Freeman Asian Cultural Experience at Sewanee (FACES). A two-week, tuition-free program in Asian studies. Prefers students entering twelfth grade. The University of the South (Sewanee) is a selective liberal arts college in rural Tennessee. Deadline: March 15. More Information: www.sewanee.edu

Telluride Association Summer Programs. One of the nation's most prestigious summer programs. Six-week seminars focus on thematic issues in the humanities and social sciences. Locations include Cornell University and University of Michigan. Nomination required in

December. Deadline: January 16. More information: www.tellurideassociation.org

Wabash College. Opportunities to Learn about Business. Open to rising twelfth graders, this weeklong program is ideal for students considering a business major. Wabash is a small, all-male liberal arts college in Indiana. (The program is co-ed.) Deadline: April 15. More information: www.wabash.edu/olab

Minority Students

Carleton College. Liberal Arts Experience. Open to students between tenth and eleventh grades, the program lasts for one week and pays for all expenses, including travel. Carleton is a highly selective liberal arts college in Minnesota. Deadline: Nomination by March 1. More information: www.carleton.edu/admissions/CLAE

Carnegie Mellon University. Summer Programs for Diversity. Offers six weeks of study for students in underrepresented groups who are interested in science and math. CMU is one of the nation's premier technically oriented universities. Open to students who have completed grades ten

or eleven. Deadline: April 1. More information: www.cmu.edu

Massachusetts Institute of Technology. Minority Introduction to Engineering, Entrepreneurship, and Science. Offers six weeks of tuition-free study and all the fun of Boston in the summer. Open to students who have finished grade eleven. Attendees must pay transportation costs. Deadline: early February. More information: www.mit.edu

Quest Scholars Program. A small, highly competitive program that offers a five-week summer program and five years of subsequent mentorship to low-income, at-risk students. Based at Stanford and open to students who have completed grade eleven. Deadline: early spring. More information: questscholars.stanford.edu

> I reminded my son that for several of his colleges, the earlier he applied, the earlier he would hear back, and that appealed to him.
>
> —**University of Southern California mom**

Telluride Association Sophomore Seminars. Six-week program open to African Americans that focuses on topics relevant to the black experience. Small and highly competitive. Nomination required in December. Deadline: January 10. More information: www.tellurideassociation.org

Noteworthy

Boston University, Institute for Television, Film, and Radio Production. Film is all the rage among today's students, and what better place to study it than Boston in the summer? This program costs a pretty penny—over $4,000—but it offers a unique opportunity for students interested in film. Deadline: March 30. More information: www.bu.edu/com/itrp

Concordia Language Villages. Serving nearly ten thousand students per year, Concordia offers the finest in summer language instruction and is available for students in grades three to twelve. Languages include Chinese, Danish, Finnish, French, German, Italian, Japanese, Korean, Norwegian, Russian, Spanish, and Swedish. Deadline: spring. More information: clvweb.cord.edu

Eleanor Roosevelt Center at Val-Kill. Girls' Leadership workshop. A nine-day program for girls who will enter grades 10 or 11 that includes a diverse assortment of themes ranging from citizenship to the arts. Requires a token fee of $200. Deadline: February 28. More Information: www.ervk.org

> Often colleges "reconsider" financial aid awards. Private colleges tend not to match public costs, though we did have one family who asked and had Stanford match the in-state tuition of University of Colorado.
>
> **—Counselor's heads-up**

Landmark Volunteers. Offers two weeks of community service in places ranging from Acadia National Park in Maine to Golden Gate National Recreation Area in California. Open to students in the summer after grades nine, ten, or eleven. Fee in the form of a tax-deductible $875 contribution. Deadline: March 31. More information: www.volunteers.com

> Pay attention to which schools offer merit awards. One friend told me she was sure her son would get a merit scholarship to Dartmouth because he was so exceptional, but Dartmouth doesn't give merit awards to anyone.
>
> —University of Southern California mom

Massachusetts Institute of Technology. Women's Technology Program. Not free, but at a cost of only $1,000 for six weeks, the WTP is definitely a bargain. Open to students after completion of eleventh grade. Deadline: February 1. More information: www.mit.edu

U.S. Military Academies. West Point, the Naval Academy, the Air Force Academy, and the Coast Guard Academy offer low-cost, weeklong programs that provide a taste of military life. Recommended for students who are considering the academies. Deadlines: early spring. More information: Contact the academies.

New York University, Tisch Summer High School Programs. Another pricey program that makes this list because it combines world-class arts programs with Greenwich Village in the summer. Need we say more? Programs include acting, dramatic writing, musical theater, and film. Deadline: March 10. More information: www.nyu.edu

University of Notre Dame—Summer Introduction to Engineering. ND offers this three-week program for about $1,000 to students who have completed eleventh grade. Other programs include an introduction to architecture and a low-cost weeklong program for Catholics that focuses on church teachings. Deadline: early spring. More information: www.nd.edu

> Applying early-decision absolutely increases the likelihood of admission. Anyone who says it doesn't is being dishonest.
>
> —Counselor's heads-up

SEPTEMBER 2006

WITH DEADLINES LOOMING IN THE LATE FALL, smart students will use September to get into high gear. Now is the time to double-check admission requirements and confirm the fall standardized testing schedule. Students with a first-choice college should consider applying via early decision and early action. (See page 103.) Students who plan to file paper applications should call or email to request them. By late September, students should make preliminary contact with teacher recommenders. Forms and backup material can come later. Families should confirm arrangements for September and October college visits. Students are advised to check with the guidance office to find out when college representatives are visiting.

WHAT TO DO:

✓ **Wednesday, September 13**
October SAT and Subject Tests, registration deadline*

✓ **Saturday, September 16**
ACT administered

✓ **Friday, September 22**
October ACT, registration deadline

✓ **Friday, September 29**
November SAT and Subject Tests, registration deadline*

*Approximate deadline. Check with www.collegeboard.com.

SEPTEMBER 1–2, 2006

The first meaningful date on the fall calendar is August 18, the registration deadline for the September ACT. This date is offered only in **Arizona, California, Florida, Georgia, Illinois, Indiana, Maryland, Nevada, North Carolina, Pennsylvania, South Carolina, Texas,** and **Washington**.

The University of Texas fires a warning shot over the bow of the Class of 2007 by beginning its processing of housing applications. On-campus housing varies, and the best stuff fills up early. Students considering UT are strongly advised to file their housing applications by October 1 for top priority. Students can and should apply for housing before they apply for admission, though they must be accepted in order to get a housing contract. UT is an extreme case, but many state universities recommend that students apply for housing before admission. Among the places where it pays to apply for housing early are College of Charleston, University of Colorado at Boulder, University of Florida, George Washington University, University of North Carolina at Chapel Hill, North Carolina State, University of Kansas, and University of Wisconsin at Madison.

Friday, September 1

☐ University of Texas at Austin begins processing housing applications for fall 2006

Saturday, September 2

THE ANNUAL RANKINGS FRENZY

Early September marks a uniquely American ritual: the release of *U.S. News & World Report*'s annual rankings of the colleges. The original version in 1983 consisted of a poll of university presidents. *U.S. News* has continued to revise its formula on a regular basis since then.

> For a West Coast "geo" applicant, we've found that Eastern liberal arts colleges are more accepting of early-decision applicants than those from the regular applicant pool.
>
> —Counselor's heads-up

College administrators continue to disdain the rankings—unless their college happens to place highly, in which case they hustle out a news release trumpeting the results. An important factor in today's rankings of national institutions is what *U.S. News* calls "peer assessment," a survey of presidents, provosts, and deans of admission wherein they are asked to rate other institutions. In a bizarre twist, administrators are now targeted by public-relations campaigns from competing institutions hoping to curry favor for the next *U.S. News* survey.

On the plus side, the rankings give a good indication of the prestige and selectivity of institutions nationwide, and the regional lists can help families identify options that might have been overlooked. In the body of its college issue, *U.S. News* generally has better reporting, we think, than its major college-issue rivals produced by *Time* and *Newsweek*. But the numeric rank order should be taken with a full shaker of salt; there is simply no way to pigeon-hole institutions as big and complex as universities into a precise numerical scale.

The rankings frenzy would be comical if it weren't such a high-stakes game. A decline can send alumni into an uproar, while an advance can signal that a college is "on-the-move." Small wonder that the colleges form committees and conduct studies to find out what determines the rankings and how they can package their numbers to look better. As long as the *U.S. News* college issue keeps flying off the shelves, the jockeying for position will continue.

SEPTEMBER 3–9, 2006

If you haven't already done so, the Labor Day weekend would be a great time to get your testing schedule straight for the fall. The registration deadline for the October SAT comes next week, with the deadline for the October ACT close on its heels. If early decision or action is in your future, these are the last dates guaranteed to be in time. Mid- to late September is also a good time to continue college visits. Don't go in early September because the first-year students are still settling in, and be wary of mid-October because that is when college midterm exams hit (and when high school work begins to get tough). The PSAT deadline for students with disabilities applies to high school counselors, who must forward forms by this date for every student they believe deserves testing with accommodations. In order to do so, they must have the proper documentation from parents. (See page xix.)

Sunday, September 3

_____   _____

_____   _____

Monday, September 4

_____   _____

_____   _____

Tuesday, September 5

_____   _____

_____   _____

Wednesday, September 6

☐ Students with disabilities, deadline to apply for
accommodations on the PSAT

_____

Thursday, September 7

Friday, September 8

Saturday, September 9

SEPTEMBER 10–16, 2006

The registration deadline for the October SAT highlights this week's calendar. At midweek, the names of about sixteen thousand National Merit Semifinalists are announced to the media, though most qualifying students will probably be notified a few days earlier by their schools. (See page 24.) Semifinalists have just under a month to complete their Finalist applications, which include an essay, grade report, and recommendation. Semifinalists must also take an SAT on one of the designated dates and send an official report to National Merit.

If you're going to need teacher recommendations, this week would be a great time to ask. Some teachers get swamped with requests, and asking early can move you to the front of the line. (See page 109.) The ACT is offered this week only in the states listed on page 221.

Sunday, September 10

_____   _____

_____   _____

Monday, September 11

_____   _____

_____   _____

Tuesday, September 12

_____   _____

_____   _____

Wednesday, September 13

☐ October SAT and Subject Tests, registration
deadline (approximate)

_____

Thursday, September 14

☐ Public Announcement of National Merit
Semifinalists

_____

Friday, September 15

Saturday, September 16

☐ ACT Administered in some states

THE JEFFERSON AND MOREHEAD MERIT SCHOLARSHIPS

Not your run-of-the-mill merit scholarships are these. The Jefferson Scholars program is the University of Virginia's premier competition, and the Morehead is a similar program at University of North Carolina at Chapel Hill. Both are based solely on merit, and both cover the complete costs of attendance plus a summer stipend. Given that UVA and UNC are two of the nation's most selective public universities (especially for out-of-state students), the competition for these scholarships is somewhere between intense and insane. Both competitions are open to students who attend in-state high schools—Jefferson by nomination and Morehead by application. In addition, both programs allow nominations from selected out-of-state high schools with good enough connections to be included. Students not attending one of these schools have the possibility of consideration on an at-large basis. Whether or not you attend a participating school, don't even give it a second thought unless you have some heady credentials. The nomination process takes place in September and October at the designated schools. Here are some other ultracompetitive scholarships that rival these, with the application deadlines:

- University of Chicago, College Honor Scholarship: full tuition, January 1

- Duke University, Angier B. Duke Scholarship: full tuition and summer stipend, January 1

- Emory University, Emory Scholars: up to full costs, November 1

- Wake Forest University, Reynolds Scholarship: full expenses and summer stipend, December 1

- Washington & Lee University, George Washington Honor Scholarships: full tuition, December 15

- Washington University (MO), Danforth Scholarship: full tuition, October 15, nomination required.

THE EARLY GAME: TO PLAY OR NOT TO PLAY

Applying early is all the rage in college admission. A recent book by two Harvard professors and a former Wesleyan admission officer says that applying via early decision has the same effect as adding nearly two hundred points to a student's SAT score, while early action gives the equivalent of a one-hundred-point boost. Some college officials, notably the dean of admission at Harvard, have disputed those numbers, but no one can deny that applying early gives many students a boost.

In early admission, terminology is crucial. Early decision (ED) entails a binding commitment to enroll if accepted. Early decision deadlines begin October 1 and continue through January, with some colleges offering two deadlines for ED consideration. Early action, a more benign program, gives students the benefit of an early yea or nay without the commitment to attend.

ED is controversial because colleges use it to manipulate their admission numbers so as to appear more selective. Students get the short end of the deal, losing about five months of additional time to weigh their options. ED makes sense for a student who is angling for admission at a "reach" school and who has no financial need. By throwing themselves at the college's mercy, these students have better odds of getting a fat letter. Students with financial need, or students who are confident of getting in, may be better served by keeping their options open and maintaining their ability to compare aid and scholarship offers.

Colleges have been roundly criticized for clinging to ED, and a few stout-hearted places like Yale, Stanford, and University of North Carolina at Chapel Hill have eliminated it in favor of more student-friendly early action. (The hitch: Many of these places, including Yale and Stanford, don't allow you to apply early to any other schools when you apply early to them.)

Despite the pitfalls, applying ED will continue to make sense for some students. If you're a borderline applicant to a highly selective school and don't need aid, consider it. Otherwise, be wary. For a complete analysis of early decision and early action, consult the *Fiske Guide to Getting into the Right College*.

SEPTEMBER 17–23, 2006

Ah, late September. The mornings are crisp, a hint of fall is in the air, and the sun still shines warmly. A perfect time to kick back and relax? Not if you're smart. There are storm clouds on the horizon called October, November, and December, and when they roll in, you'll be pelted with papers, exams, and application deadlines.

If you are lucky enough to have a late-September lull, use it. The last two weeks of September are a perfect time to get at least one of your applications DONE. Some hard work now will take the pressure off later.

Make sure that the registration deadline for the November SAT does not sneak up on you. The deadline is next week even though the calendar still says September. Davidson's **Bryan Scholars** program is one of the most prestigious for that endangered species, the scholar/athlete. One of the nation's elite small colleges, **Davidson** makes available two of these full-tuition awards.

Sunday, September 17

Monday, September 18

Tuesday, September 19

_____   _____

_____   _____

Wednesday, September 20

☐ October SAT, late-registration deadline
(approximate)

☐ Davidson College, Bryan Scholars deadline

_____   _____

Thursday, September 21

_____   _____

_____   _____

Friday, September 22

☐ October ACT, registration deadline

_____   _____

_____   _____

Saturday, September 23

_____   _____

_____   _____

SEPTEMBER 24–30, 2006

This week's primary deadline is for the November SAT. Many students use this date for one more crack at the Subject Tests after taking their last SAT in October. Even at colleges that don't require Subject Tests, a good score will be a plus. And one more reminder: Make sure you do some prep. Since the Subject Tests cover specific subject matter, the odds are good that preparation can improve your score.

The **QuestBridge College Match** program assists low-income students in applying for admission and scholarships at more than a dozen participating institutions, a sampling of which includes **Amherst, University of North Carolina at Chapel Hill, Princeton**, and **Rice**.

Sunday, September 24

Monday, September 25

☐ QuestBridge College Match. www.questbridge.org

Tuesday, September 26

Wednesday, September 27

_____   _____
_____   _____
_____   _____

Thursday, September 28

_____   _____
_____   _____
_____   _____

Friday, September 29

☐ November SAT and Subject Tests, registration   _____
   deadline (approximate)   _____

_____   _____

Saturday, September 30

_____   _____
_____   _____
_____   _____

Much of the confusion in college admission comes from the fact that half of the colleges are trying to appear less selective than they really are, and the other half are trying to appear more selective than they really are.

Highly selective schools revel in their reputations for choosiness, but there is a problem. If students think that they have no hope of admission at the Princetons of the world, they won't bother to apply, and Princeton will lose applicants. Like all the other highly selective schools, Princeton wants borderline applicants to apply, not because significant numbers of them will get in, but because the fact that they won't get in will feed Princeton's aura as a highly selective school. If a typical B+ student goes to a session with a Princeton admission officer, will that student come away feeling as if he or she has a shot at getting in? In many cases, yes. Is it a realistic possibility? Probably not.

On the other side, consider Ithaca College, which recently noted on its website that "Typically, some 11,000 men and women apply for 1,550 places in the freshman class." Does this mean that Ithaca is accepting about one in ten applicants? Not exactly. In this passage, which appeared on its website under the heading of "Just the Facts," Ithaca left out the fact that it admits about 6,000 applicants in order to get those 1,550 to enroll. Ithaca is one of the many, many colleges that tries to make itself look more selective than it really is.

Rule of thumb: Assume that your odds for admission are lower than you might think after that wonderful meeting with the Princeton rep, and that your odds are higher than you would be led to believe from a session with an Ithaca admission officer.

> The admission process is about finding the place where you belong, not about portraying yourself in an artificial manner in order to be accepted at a certain school.
>
> —University of Kansas student

ROUNDING UP TEACHER RECOMMENDERS

Late September is an ideal time for students to contact teacher recommenders. But will you actually do it? Probably not. Students love to procrastinate on this one. They wait and wait—sometimes until the week before winter vacation—then spring the recommendation request on a harried teacher who is already juggling ten other letters. Memo to students: You don't need to wait until you have all the application forms in hand to ask.

There is no great trick to getting a letter. An English teacher is the most logical choice—no subject is more central to a student's academic experience, and English teachers tend to be good writers. Alternatively, students may choose a history, social studies, or foreign language teacher. For balance, students generally combine one of these with a math or science teacher. Teachers from yearbook, art, or other non-core courses should generally be avoided. (If the arts are a particularly important part of your life, consider getting an additional recommendation from an art teacher to supplement the ones in core academic subjects.)

A teacher who can speak to the student's academic and personal qualities will typically do the best job. Some parents think they can work the system by contacting the close friend of their brother-in-law who happens to be on the board of First Choice U, or by getting a recommendation from the state senator who got a campaign contribution from Dad. By and large, these attempts at small-time influence peddling fall flat. If your family name is on the college library, that's big-time influence peddling, which will work just fine.

Students should be sure to give their teachers plenty of backup material on writing the recommendations. A note summarizing the student's experiences with the teacher—including references to particular assignments—would be helpful. (When teachers have one hundred students in their classes, it is possible to know a student well and still need a memory jog.) Copies of papers on which you did well would be a major bonus. An activity chart would also be helpful, and, of course, the necessary forms with the student's information filled out at the top. Schools vary in their procedures for mailing recommendations, but if mailing the letter is the teacher's responsibility, it is courteous to include stamped envelopes. Most important, students should emphasize the date of their earliest deadline and politely check back a week before to make sure the recommendation is in the pipeline.

When Admission Officers Come to School

College admission officers spend the winter and spring reviewing applications. What do they do in the fall? Many of them can be seen at a high school near you. Admission offices typically divide the country into regions, with particular staff members responsible for each area. Private colleges generally send representatives to all corners of the nation during the fall; public institutions usually limit their visits to contiguous states. Some colleges visit the same high school every year. Others will visit every other year, while still others hold group information sessions at local venues in lieu of high school visits.

Check in at the guidance office for a list of the representatives who will visit, and keep checking back because the schedule is subject to change.

Keep in mind that the representative who visits will probably be the first one to read your application. Even if the family has already visited the college and had an interview, students should make the effort to meet the regional representative at their school. Colleges count contacts, and the more a student has expressed interest, the better his or her chances are for admission.

Might a thank-you note be in order after the visit? Great idea—but few students ever write one. If you can't attend the session, write a note expressing regrets or get the representative's email address from the college counselor. Colleges know that students can't always get out of class—making the effort to follow up is what counts.

For Parents: Top Five Signs of a Procrastination Emergency

5. Your son or daughter becomes testy when you suggest that four hours per day on the phone with friends may be too much.

4. Homework mysteriously becomes a top priority when you bring up the subject of college applications.

3. Son claims that he is spending three hours per night chatting with admission officers via AOL Instant Messenger.

2. Daughter refuses to discuss her college essay but insists that it is "almost done."

1. Son appears unaware that there is a deadline to apply for admission.

For procrastination coping strategies, see page 37.

OCTOBER 2006

OCTOBER IS WHEN EVERYTHING HITS THE FAN. Early applications at the most selective colleges should be filed by the end of this month. Students should complete their application lists and make a last check of their transcripts. Early October is the best time to firm up a game plan with the college counselor. Teacher recommenders should be confirmed. Financial aid applicants at highly selective colleges should complete the CSS/PROFILE form where necessary.

The Class of 2008 gets a taste of the college admission process with the administration of the PSAT. For a less stressful way to stick a toe in the water, juniors should sit in on meetings at school with visiting college representatives. See your the guidance counselor to find out the schedule.

WHAT TO DO:

✓ **Saturday, October 14**
SAT and Subject Tests administered

✓ **Sunday, October 15**
Early-action and scholarship deadlines

✓ **Wednesday, October 18
and Saturday, October 21**
PSAT administered

✓ **Friday, October 27**
December SAT, registration
deadline*

✓ **Saturday, October 28**
ACT administered

*Approximate deadline. Check with www.collegeboard.com.

OCTOBER 1–7, 2006

October means that things are getting serious. The November SAT date is a close shave for early-decision or early-action programs, but scores from this date often get in there under the wire. (The prize for the nation's earliest early decision deadline goes to the **University of Florida** and its October 1 deadline.) National Merit semifinalists must turn in their applications for Finalist by a high-school-specific deadline, usually this week. A letter of recommendation is required for each Finalist application, so don't be surprised if the college counselor has a slightly glazed look. The College Board swings into action with its CSS/PRO-FILE form, a supplement to the Free Application for Federal Student Aid (FAFSA), which is used by some selective private colleges. Students must register for it online. We recommend that students wait until their list of colleges is fairly firm before registering for the PROFILE. Since there are various questions that colleges require at their discretion, the form varies depending on where the student applies. The final deadline for the **NFAA ARTS** competition is also this week. The **Hispanic Scholarship Fund** teams up with **Toyota** to offer scholarships of up to $5,000 to students who attend one of six leading public institutions in California or Texas and major in selected fields. **Siemens Westinghouse** is a famous math and science project-based competition that awards scholarships that total up to $100,000 over four years. One unique program not on the calendar is the **Wells Fargo College STEPS Program,** which awards ten scholarships of $1,000 each month via random drawings that begin in October. For more information, head to www.wellsfargo.com.

Sunday, October 1

- ☐ University of Florida, early-decision deadline
- ☐ CSS/PROFILE Online Application Available

- ☐ NFAA ARTS final deadline. www.artsawards.org
- ☐ Hispanic Scholarship Fund/Toyota Motors. www.hsf.net/scholarships.php

Monday, October 2

☐ Siemens Westinghouse Competition.
www.siemens-foundation.org

Tuesday, October 3

Wednesday, October 4

Thursday, October 5

Friday, October 6

☐ October ACT, late-registration deadline

☐ National Merit Finalist applications,
approximate due date

Saturday, October 7

What's in an Application?

It's really very simple. A college application includes four parts:

- **The student's section.** Includes basic personal information, a list of activities and honors, short essays about meaningful activities and/or why the student is interested in the college, and a more extended personal statement.

- **The secondary school report.** Asks the college counselor to evaluate the applicant with an essay and with check-offs about rigor of curriculum and personal qualities ranging from initiative to sense of humor.

- **The teacher recommendation.** A teacher's assessment of the student's strengths and weaknesses.

- **Test scores.** Generally reported from the testing agency at the request of the student, though sometimes also on the back of the transcript and in the student's part of the application.

Each section has a corresponding piece of paper (or two), and keeping track of these can be a big job. Online filers will submit the student's section electronically, but such students will still need to print the relevant forms for the counselor and teachers or give them paper copies. The counselor and teacher forms often have detailed check-off ratings that ask if the student is a) "one of the top few I have taught," b) "one of the best this year," or c) excellent (top 10 percent this year), and so on. But many school personnel bridle at completing these ratings and simply say "see attached" and clip their essay. A growing number of schools have designed their own secondary-school report forms and have dispensed with doing a different one for each college.

As the fall progresses, students should keep this in mind: The sooner they can get the appropriate forms to teachers and counselors, the sooner their applications are likely to be processed.

> The admission process seems more about the colleges and their "image" than it does about the student and the best match for them.
>
> —Counselor's heads-up

A Last Check of the Transcript

Parents and students have a right to see the transcript before it is sent out, and smart ones won't let the opportunity pass. First, check for mistakes, which are all too common. One hapless applicant to the University of Texas found out the hard way when he mailed his application and his counselor sent the transcript with an incorrect social security number. As do many large institutions, UT sorts applications by social security number. The transcript was stuck in la-la land for several months before the error was finally discovered. There are numerous questions students and parents should ask about the student's transcript:

- Does it include honors or activities? Some do, most don't. If so, does it include any the student has forgotten about?

- Are summer courses listed? The grade? Usually so, though awarding of credit varies.

- What about courses from previous schools? Has the school transferred all your credits?

- Which test scores are on there? Some schools report test scores on the back, others don't. Make sure the right scores are there.

The test score issue is particularly touchy because some students have scores they don't want to send. Some schools put the PSAT on the transcript—but if the score wasn't among the student's best, ask the school to take it off. AP scores can also be withheld at your discretion. If the student took both the ACT and SAT, one can be sent and the other withheld if the applicant so chooses.

Usually, a cumulative GPA is on the transcript, and schools have various ways of calculating them. Many weigh honors and AP courses. For instance, if an A is equal to 4.0 under normal circumstances, it might be worth a 4.33 or even 5.0 on a weighted scale. Methods vary. Some high schools omit arts courses from the GPA; many omit phys ed. A GPA is meaningful only in relative terms, so don't worry about the boy across town who has a 4.8 at Crosstown High when the best possible GPA at your school is a 4.0. Bear in mind that many colleges recalculate GPAs according to their own criteria, and a few shave off ninth grade for a closer look at recent work.

INSIDE THE PSAT

The Class of 2008 gets its first meaningful introduction to college admission with the Preliminary SAT. Some schools choose to administer it during a school day—this year the date is Wednesday, October 18—and others do it on Saturday, October 21. The PSAT is an abbreviated version of the SAT that many students will have taken once before as tenth graders. This time, the results count in the National Merit competition, which gives recognition and a chance at scholarships to just under 5 percent of the eleventh-grade test-takers. (See page 24 for details.)

In 2004, the PSAT underwent similar though less sweeping changes as those on the new SAT. The old verbal section was renamed Critical Reading, the analogy questions were dropped, and more reading passages were added. The Math and Writing Skills sections are largely unchanged, though the Algebra and Geometry sections will be slightly more challenging than in the past to better reflect the math that students cover through tenth grade. As before, there is no essay on the PSAT. (For more on the new SAT, see page 42.)

Unlike the SAT and ACT, the PSAT is a school-based test and generally students are automatically signed up to take it. If in doubt, check to make sure. Students who are homeschooled should contact a local high school and arrange to take the test there. Students occasionally have problems if their school arranges a Saturday administration that conflicts with an athletic contest or other event. Students are allowed to take the test at a school other than their own, and students with conflicts on Saturday should investigate local schools that may be giving it on Wednesday. Unfortunately, there is no way to make up the PSAT. Students who miss it can qualify for the National Merit Scholarship Competition with a high score on the SAT.

FOR PARENTS: ANOTHER CHORUS OF THE PROCRASTINATION BLUES

So you followed our advice in the spring and it didn't work, eh? Son or daughter is still in major denial and you don't know what to do? Don't panic, and try to distinguish between serious paralysis and the garden-variety avoidance that is rampant at this time of the year, even among high-functioning kids.

The surest sign of real trouble is when nothing is happening: Your son or daughter shows no effort to get applications, doesn't show up at college visits, and generally is not engaged in the process. If that sounds familiar, you're probably at wit's end with how to deal.

We can imagine the scenario. You suggest working on applications. Nothing happens. You say no more TV or computer until applications are done. Still nothing. You declare a lockdown until applications are done. More avoidance.

Clearly, you and your child are now at loggerheads. Any push from you will provoke an equal and opposite push back. Although your son or daughter may be wearing a mask of indifference, their real message is that the burden of everything—college applications, leaving home, figuring out what to do with the rest of their lives—has become too much for them to deal with productively. They don't need to be told what to do; they need active assistance in doing it.

Break the adversarial dynamic and become an ally. Help make a list of major deadlines. Sit down together and begin work on applications. You'll probably encounter some resistance, so be low-key but persistent. Help organize and set priorities but let the student do the real work. Once the ball is rolling, look for opportunities to pull back.

One other thought: Suggest a college visit with a friend. This can be delicate, but if a friend of your child is looking at some of the same colleges, encourage them to make a visit together or with you. Harnessing the benign impact of peers is especially useful for boys who have girlfriends. You may not want them going to the same college, but the chances are good that the girlfriend is much further ahead in looking at colleges.

We wish we could say that these strategies are foolproof—you know they're not. Procrastination is a tough nut to crack. If all else fails, remind yourself that everything will ultimately work out. Young people find their way in life through a variety of paths. Your child will be no exception.

OCTOBER 8–14, 2006

Welcome to the last week of sanity before the final early-decision scramble. Anyone seeking help with applications or essays will receive a warmer reception in the guidance office this week than they will later in the month. Ditto for contacting teacher recommenders. If asking for a recommendation has, er, slipped your mind or if you have decided at the last minute to apply early, we recommend that you bring flowers or candy along with the form.

This week is also a good time to get serious about the scholarship search. Many require paperwork from teachers or the guidance office. Turn in forms and ask for recommendations at least three weeks in advance.

Early-decision and early-action applicants who plan to apply for financial aid at colleges requiring the CSS/PROFILE should register to receive the form at www.collegeboard.com and file by November 1.

Sunday, October 8

_____   _____
_____   _____
_____   _____

Monday, October 9

_____   _____
_____   _____
_____   _____

Tuesday, October 10

_____

_____

_____

Wednesday, October 11

☐ November SAT and Subject Tests, late-registration
deadline (approximate)

_____

Thursday, October 12

_____   _____

_____   _____

_____   _____

Friday, October 13

_____   _____

_____   _____

_____   _____

Saturday, October 14

_____   _____

_____   _____

_____   _____

OCTOBER 15–21, 2006

Any week with a **Harvard** deadline is serious business. Although Harvard's early-action deadline is only "recommended" (with November 1 required), smart applicants will mail their materials by October 15. Note that Harvard, like **Yale** and **Stanford**, forbids early-action applicants from applying ED or EA anywhere else. **Boston University** administers a multiple-choice test in late October on its campus, and at participating high schools, for scholarships up to full tuition in its College of Engineering. Washington University's **Danforth Scholarship**, also up to full tuition, requires a school nomination. Whittier College's deadline is for its Honors Weekend, when it parcels out scholarships worth up to the full cost of attendance.

The **Horatio Alger Scholarship Program** offers one hundred one-time scholarships of $10,000 and another two hundred awards of $1,000 to students with financial need who have overcome obstacles. The **Outstanding Students of America** organization bestows ten one-time scholarships of up to $10,000 with an emphasis on community service.

Sunday, October 15

- ☐ Harvard University, University of Georgia, early action deadline

- ☐ George Washington University, early-decision deadline (part one)

- ☐ Boston University—Scholarship Examination Competition. www.bu.edu

- ☐ Washington University (MO), Danforth Scholars. www.wustl.edu

- ☐ Whittier College Honors Weekend Deadline. www.whittier.edu

- ☐ Outstanding Students of America Scholarship. www.outstandingstudentsofamerica.com

- ☐ Horatio Alger Scholarship Program. www.horatioalger.com

Monday, October 16

Tuesday, October 17

Wednesday, October 18

☐ PSAT Administered

Thursday, October 19

Friday, October 20

Saturday, October 21

☐ PSAT Administered

OCTOBER 22–31, 2006

If you think the odds are long at **Harvard** or **Stanford,** try the annual Coca-Cola Scholars competition, where about 100,000 students apply for 250 one-time scholarships of up to $20,000. The **Prudential Spirit of Community Awards** are only slightly less competitive, with a school nomination required to compete for sixty one-time scholarships of up to $6,000. The **Georgia Tech Presidential Scholarship** covers the full costs of attendance for top students who want to join the Ramblin' Wreck.

D-Day for most early-application filers is around the corner. At the beginning of the week, these students should politely check with teachers and counselors to make sure everything is in order. (By Wednesday, the college counselor is likely to be in the middle of a stress meltdown.) This week marks the registration deadline for the December SAT and Subject Tests—the last date when scores are guaranteed to arrive in time for regular-decision consideration at selective and highly selective institutions. Students use this date to finish off the Subject Tests or take one more stab at the SAT.

Sunday, October 22

_____

_____

_____

Monday, October 23

_____

_____

_____

Tuesday, October 24

_____

_____

_____

Wednesday, October 25

_____

_____

_____

Thursday, October 26

_____
_____
_____

Friday, October 27

☐ December SAT, registration deadline (approximate)
☐ CSS PROFILE begins sending reports to the colleges

_____

Saturday, October 28

_____
_____
_____

_____
_____
_____

Sunday, October 29

_____
_____
_____

_____
_____
_____

Monday, October 30

_____
_____
_____
_____

Tuesday, October 31

☐ Prudential Spirit of Community Awards.
www.principals.org
☐ Georgia Tech President's Scholarship.
www.gatech.edu
☐ Coca-Cola Scholars. www.coca-colascholars.org

TEN SIGNS THAT THE COLLEGE RAT RACE IS OUT OF CONTROL

Parents aren't the only ones who get stressed out over the college search. By late fall of twelfth grade, the whole family may be losing its grip on reality. Here are some warning signs:

10. Son ignores State Department travel warning in order to seek résumé-building community service experience among Kurdish separatists near the Iraq–Turkey border.

9. Daughter complains that classmate who uses a wheelchair has better college essay topic.

8. Son is distressed to learn that the SAT does not offer extra-credit problems.

7. Mom has a sudden falling out with best friend after the friend's daughter is accepted early at Yale.

6. Dad proclaims that only SAT vocabulary words may be used in dinner conversations.

5. The family hires a private investigator to verify that the student's great-great-grandfather was half Cherokee.

4. Thanksgiving dinner conversation is devoted to critiquing essay drafts.

3. Daughter memorizes Tiers I and II of the *U.S. News* National University rankings.

2. Mom searches the Web for a car-window decal that says "also accepted at . . ."

1. The message on the family answering machine notes that daughter is National Merit Semifinalist.

NOVEMBER 2006

PRIME TIME CONTINUES FOR FILING APPLICATIONS. Most early-decision and early-action deadlines are in November, and students should also file applications at colleges with rolling admission. (These colleges evaluate applications continuously and typically offer a decision in about one month.)

After filing applications, early applicants should log on to the college's website to make sure their applications are complete. After a quick breather, early birds should focus on filing additional applications. (See page 140.) Paper copies of the Free Application for Federal Student Aid (FAFSA) should be available late this month. We recommend that students complete a paper copy and then use it to file online.

WHAT TO DO:

✓ **Wednesday, November 1**
Early-decision, early-action, and institutional scholarship deadlines

✓ **Friday, November 3**
December ACT, registration deadline

✓ **Saturday, November 4**
SAT and Subject Tests administered

✓ **Wednesday, November 15**
Early-decision, early-action, and institutional scholarship deadlines

NOVEMBER 1–4, 2006

November 1 begins the deadline season in earnest. Institutions with early-decision deadlines include **Boston University, Brown, Dartmouth, Emory, Rice**, and **Wellesley**, among others. Early-action deadlines are at **Caltech, Georgetown, James Madison, MIT, SMU**, and **Tulane**. Fifteen full-tuition scholarships are up for grabs to early applicants at **Boston College**, and **North Carolina State** offers sixty scholarships that cover the full cost of attendance. **Miami University of Ohio** has a November 1 deadline for its full-ride **Harrison Scholarship**, and **Rhodes College** requires a nomination for its full-tuition **Bellingrath Scholarship**. Other colleges with a scholarship deadline of November 1 include **University of Kansas, Michigan State, Scripps, University of Tennessee**, and **Villanova University**. (For a complete list of November deadlines, see Appendix B.)

The **Target All-Around Scholarship** competition is among the nation's richest, offering more than 600 one-time awards of $1,000 and a grand prize of $25,000. The **VFW Voice of Democracy** competition bestows fifty one-time awards up to $5,000. Students in grades 9–12 may enter the competition with a

Wednesday, November 1

☐ Early-decision and early-action deadlines

☐ Institutional merit scholarship deadlines

☐ VFW Voice of Democracy Scholarship. www.vfw.org

☐ Target All-Around Scholarship.
http://target.com/target_group/
community_giving/scholarships.jhtml

Thursday, November 2

_____

_____

_____

Friday, November 3

☐ December ACT, registration deadline

Saturday, November 4

☐ SAT and Subject Tests administered

ESSAY HELP: HOW MUCH IS TOO MUCH?

It was a sign of the times when Duke University asked applicants to the Class of 2007 if they had received help on their essays. (Ninety-five percent said they had.) Skepticism of essays written like E. B. White by kids with grades like George W. Bush has been growing in recent years. Was it Mom who wrote with such flourish about how you dove and caught the ball? Did Dad's secretary polish it up? Which ideas were the student's, and which came from the college counselor?

There is nothing wrong with offering help on an essay. Here are some perfectly legitimate ways for parents to assist:

- **Probing for a topic.** Some students have a hard time with self-disclosure. Parents can help steer them toward a topic they can make their own.

- **Organization, word choice, and grammar.** There is nothing wrong with flagging common errors, or suggesting that the student look again at how the piece is organized.

- **Proofread, proofread, proofread.** Students are anxious about writing their essay, and as a result they want to get it done as fast as possible. Many an essay is marred with careless errors. Parents should strongly recommend that the student show them the final draft before mailing it out, or that they set it aside and then proof it one more time.

So where is the line? We draw a bright one at the point where a parent becomes tempted to write the essay rather than simply raising issues and pointing out mistakes. If you find yourself composing sentences, take a deep breath and several steps back. For a complete overview of the college essay, consult the *Fiske Guide to Getting into the Right College.*

NOVEMBER 5–11, 2006

In case the procrastination-busters still haven't worked, this week is the last deadline for the last SAT and Subject Tests that will be in time for most selective colleges. Applications and essays should be well under way, and all teacher recommenders should be lined up.

The **Susan G. Komen Breast Cancer Foundation** grants five one-time scholarships of $10,000 to students who have lost a parent to breast cancer.

Sunday, November 5

Monday, November 6

Tuesday, November 7

Wednesday, November 8

☐ December SAT and Subject Tests, late-registration deadline (approximate)

Thursday, November 9

Friday, November 10

☐ Elon University, early-action deadline

Saturday, November 11

☐ Susan G. Komen Breast Cancer Foundation College Scholarship Award. www.komen.org/grants

NOVEMBER 12–18, 2006

This week's early-decision deadlines include **Barnard, Bowdoin, Carnegie Mellon, Hamilton, Mount Holyoke, Tufts,** and **Wake Forest.** Early-action deadlines include **University of Chicago, Colorado College, University of Minnesota at Morris, Pepperdine,** and **SUNY Binghamton.** (For a complete list, see Appendix B.) Deep Springs College, with its admission deadline of November 15, enrolls a grand total of twenty-five Ivy-caliber male students on a remote campus in the Southwestern desert. And at the head of a growing trend among state universities, **University of Illinois at Urbana-Champaign** has its priority regular-decision deadline this week.

Army ROTC offers full tuition and books at more than six hundred colleges and universities in exchange for a commitment to serve after graduation. The **Intel Science Talent Search,** now more than sixty years old, was sponsored by Westinghouse until 1998. Five finalists have gone on to win the Nobel Prize. The Talent Search offers 340 scholarships to those who complete a scientific research project of not more than twenty pages. The grand prize of $100,000 is one of the richest of any contest in the nation.

Sunday, November 12

_____

_____

Monday, November 13

_____

_____

Tuesday, November 14

_____

_____

_____

_____

_____

_____

Wednesday, November 15

- ☐ Early-decision and early-action deadlines
- ☐ Deep Springs College, admission deadline
- ☐ University of Illinois at Urbana-Champaign, priority admission deadline
- ☐ Institutional merit scholarship deadlines
- ☐ Army ROTC Scholarship. www.armyrotc.com

_____

Thursday, November 16

- ☐ Intel Science Talent Search. www.sciserv.org/sts
- ☐ December ACT, late-registration deadline

_____

_____

_____

_____

Friday, November 17

_____

_____

_____

_____

_____

_____

Saturday, November 18

_____

_____

_____

_____

_____

_____

THE APPLICATION: ONLINE VERSUS PAPER

In the days when computers occupied entire rooms instead of desktops, students spent most of the fall chasing down paper applications from the colleges where they wanted to apply. It was a fun little game: 1) Student called the college. 2) College said it would send the application. 3) Weeks passed, no application. 4) Student called again. 5) College said it would send application again. 6) Weeks passed and still no application.

A sizable contingent of students still applies via paper applications, but more students every year send their applications with a key stroke rather than a stamp. The convenience can't be beat. Online applications still get printed out and read the old-fashioned way, but colleges prefer them because they are easier to process than the snail-mail variety. Many colleges offer incentives to apply online, such as a waiver of the application fee. The majority of applicants to state universities apply online. Applicants to selective colleges have been more reluctant to jump on the bandwagon, though their numbers are growing every year. Pitfalls of applying online can include:

- Potential loss of data due to a computer malfunction

- Inability to see the printed version as the admission office will see it

- The impulse to hit "send" before the application has been thoroughly proofread

- The fact that transcripts and recommendations must be sent separately

- Inability to amend the form or include attachments

None of these issues represent a real barrier to a smart applicant. The most important thing is to print the application before sending it—four or five times if necessary to get it just right. Additional material can always be sent through the mail. The paper-versus-electronic dilemma is really about comfort level. Old fogies like Mom and Dad would probably still prefer to use paper, while the X-Box generation is happy to use the computer.

COLLEGE ESSAYS ONLINE: ANOTHER MORAL DILEMMA

Movie buffs remember the scene in Casablanca when Claude Raines was shocked—*shocked*—to learn that gambling was going on in Rick's Cafe. That motif has been updated by the various online purveyors of college essays who are fueling concerns that today's admission offices are getting the best college essays money can buy.

> Make it easy for the college rep to remember you. Have a résumé handy in case the rep asks.
>
> —Counselor's heads-up

Consider one such outfit that we saw on the Web. It doesn't just sell editing services or sample essays; it sells packets of essays written in response to the questions at particular colleges. Applying to Princeton? Get a packet of twelve successful Princeton essays. Want to write about your athletic experiences? Buy a packet of ten essays in which successful applicants discuss how playing ball made you . . . er . . . them a better person. You can even buy a packet where various students explain the reasons why their families mean so much to them—a surefire helper if you can't think of any on your own.

The tone of the presentation turns solemn on the subject of honesty. "We absolutely do not condone plagiarism and have not created this site to encourage such behavior," says the site in its mission statement. Hmm. We'll take that statement at face value, and we admit that the line between cheating and getting ideas can be a fine one. Students will have to follow their own scruples on this issue, but be aware that every year colleges actively sniff out plagiarized or partly plagiarized essays and put their authors in the reject pile.

NOVEMBER 19–25, 2006

The Thanksgiving holiday is a good chance for students to catch their breath—or forge full speed ahead on applications. Students should plan to touch base at least once more with their counselor next week to confirm application plans and turn in any stray forms. Keep in mind how tight the December calendar will be: Counselors must file materials for all January 1 deadlines before the winter break. That leaves a scant three weeks after Thanksgiving to get everything done. Any student who decides to add an extra college to the list should inform the counselor posthaste.

The Guideposts **Young Writers Contest** offers twenty one-time awards of up to $10,000 to eleventh and twelfth graders for a first-person story about a memorable or moving experience, not to exceed 1,200 words.

Sunday, November 19

Monday, November 20

☐ Grinnell College, early-decision deadline

Tuesday, November 21

Wednesday, November 22

_____   _____

_____   _____

_____   _____

Thursday, November 23

☐ Guideposts Young Writers Contest. www.guide-   _____
posts.com/young_writers_contest.asp

_____   _____

_____   _____

Friday, November 24

_____   _____

_____   _____

_____   _____

Saturday, November 25

_____   _____

_____   _____

_____   _____

November 26–30, 2006

November 30 marks the first regular-decision deadline among major institutions. The **University of California** requires that all students apply by this date, and Penn State has its priority deadline. The National Security Agency and Defense Intelligence Agency offer renewable, full-tuition scholarships and internships to students in selected majors who agree to post-graduation employment. The DIA scholarship has an income ceiling.

Sunday, November 26

Monday, November 27

☐ Grinnell College, early-decision deadline

Tuesday, November 28

Wednesday, November 29

- [ ] University of California, admission deadline
- [ ] National Security Agency, Stokes Educational Scholarship Program www.nsa.gov

- [ ] Penn State University, priority-admission deadline
- [ ] Defense Intelligence Agency Undergraduate Training Assistance Program. www.dia.mil

THE COMMON APPLICATION CONUNDRUM

Available at www.commonapp.org, the Common Application is a form supported by over 250 colleges nationwide who agree to accept it in lieu of their own form. Participants are overwhelmingly private, though a smattering of public institutions such as Miami University (OH) and University of Maine at Orono also use the form. The idea is to cut down on paperwork by allowing students to complete only one application, photocopy it, and then send to all the colleges. In recent years, the Common App has picked up steam, with recent converts including Princeton and Yale.

Nevertheless, many high-profile institutions still do not accept the Common App, such as the University of Chicago, Columbia University, MIT, Northwestern, and Penn, to name a few. In addition, many Common App institutions continue to produce an application form of their own, though in recent years more institutions, among them Dartmouth, Harvard, and Middlebury, have chosen to use the Common exclusively.

When the college has a form of its own, is it better to use that form or is it OK to use the Common? The debate has raged back and forth. Common App schools pledge to give the applicants who use it the same consideration they give to those who use their own form. Yet some college counselors remain wary. Will college admission officers subconsciously favor their own form? Will they question the commitment of Common App applicants to their particular institution because it is so easy to reproduce? A high-profile dean of admission recently created a stir when he suggested on national television that he would not use the Common if applying to schools that have their own form.

Despite qualms such as these, students who use the Common get a fair shake nine out of ten times. Students who want to hedge their bets might apply to a first-choice college using its own form, then use the Common for other applications.

Students who use the Common should take care to make contact with admission officers and visit the campus to show that they are sincerely interested.

COMBATING DEER-IN-THE-HEADLIGHTS SYNDROME

After pouring their heart and soul into an early application, students often have a glazed look on their faces when the subject turns to working on other applications. Ideally, a student would kiss the early application good-bye, chill out for a week, and then get back to the task of applying other places. In reality, many students freeze. Everyone hopes to get a fat letter in mid-December, but those who don't should have a backup plan that does not include chasing the college counselor down the hall with five more applications on the last day before the winter break. This is where parents can be a big help.

Encourage your son or daughter not to put all their eggs in one basket. Don't get fixated on one particular school, and don't let them do it either. Stay measured and cautiously optimistic. Once the early application is in, help your son or daughter focus on other applications.

> There is much more emphasis on test scores today, contrary to how colleges try to downplay their significance.
>
> —Counselor's heads-up

As the final application push begins, it is a smart move to take one more look at the application list. If the student has a first choice college where admission is probable, the list may be only two or three schools. Applicants to selective institutions will probably want to apply to five to seven or so. Students should make sure that the mix includes at least two schools where they are likely to be admitted and at least one institution that the family can afford, with or without aid. Students who apply to two very likely schools are assured of a choice in April rather than being stuck at a lone "safety" school that may not be as appealing in April as it is in November. Most students will have no trouble identifying their dream schools, and as long as their bases are covered on the less-selective side, they should be encouraged to apply wherever their heart fancies.

It also makes sense to think again about the affordability angle. If money is an issue, consider adding a college or two where a merit scholarship might be in the cards. Sometimes these places get lost in the shuffle because they tend to be less selective than the "reach" schools that have the prestige. Students may crave being a face in the crowd at a highly selective institution, but they may get a better education at a less-known institution that gives them first-class treatment. Scholarship winners generally get the best an institution has to offer, including small honors classes, top professors, internships, research possibilities, and grooming for fellowships. Not a bad deal when you can also save money for graduate school.

> One college gave my son what amounted to an extra $3,500 discount per year—obviously a merit award, but called something else at this no-merit award Ivy institution.
>
> —Amherst College mom

DECEMBER 2006

No matter how bad December is for students, the school counselor has it worse. Students should see the counselor early—and we emphasize early—in the month with a final list of colleges. About a week before the winter break, follow up with teachers to make sure that applications are on track. Students may use the first few days of the break to finish up January 1 applications. Financial aid applicants who sat out the early round should register to receive the CSS/PROFILE form, where necessary. December is the last shot at the SAT and Subject Tests for most students, so make it a good one.

For juniors, January is the first recommended date to take the SAT Subject Tests.

WHAT TO DO:

✓ **Friday, December 1**
Early-decision, early-action, and institutional-scholarship deadlines

✓ **Saturday, December 2**
SAT and Subject Tests administered

✓ **Saturday, December 9**
ACT administered

✓ **Friday, December 15**
Early-decision, early-action, and institutional-scholarship deadlines

✓ **Thursday, December 21**
January SAT and Subject Tests, registration deadline*

*Approximate deadline. Check with www.collegeboard.com.

DECEMBER 1–2, 2005

This week's early-decision deadlines include **Austin, Drew, Earlham, Hiram, Kenyon, SUNY–Buffalo**, and **College of Wooster**. Early-action schools include **University of Connecticut, Goucher, Lawrence, Rice**, and **Willamette**. December 1 is Boston University's deadline to apply for thirty renewable, full-tuition **Trustee Scholarships**, while **Wake Forest's** Reynolds scholarship covers up to the full cost of attendance. Other institutions with scholarship deadlines include **Auburn, University of Connecticut, Millsaps, Purdue**, and **University of Texas at Austin**. (For a complete list of early-decision, early-action, and institutional-scholarship deadlines, see Appendix B.)

After years with a February admission deadline, **Marquette University** recently implemented a December 1 priority deadline for regular admission. The **University of Maryland** and **University of South Carolina**, among others, now also have priority deadlines of December 1. The **Toyota Community Scholars** program offers one hundred one-time scholarships of up to $20,000 to students nominated by their schools in early December. **Air Force ROTC** offers renewable scholarships covering full tuition plus books to students attending more than nine hundred colleges nationwide. The **Society of Automotive Engineers** offers approximately one hundred scholarships, one-time and renewable, up to full tuition.

Friday, December 1

☐ Early-decision, early-action, and regular-admission deadlines

☐ Toyota Community Scholars. www.toyota.com/about/community/education/scholars.html

☐ SAE Engineering Scholarship. www.sae.org/students/engschlr.htm

☐ Air Force ROTC Deadline. www.afrotc.com

☐ Institutional-scholarship deadlines

Saturday, December 2

☐ SAT and Subject Tests administered

Art Students Polish Their Portfolios

Students aiming for a program in the visual arts face a significantly different admission process than students in other fields, a process that can vary depending on whether they are looking for:

- An art program within a college of arts and sciences leading to a B.A.

- A B.F.A. program in an art school that is part of a comprehensive university

- A B.F.A. program in a stand-alone art school

Students should submit a portfolio in all three situations. However, arts and sciences students will be evaluated with others in the liberal arts based on grades, test scores, and so on, with the portfolio as a factor but not the whole deal.

Students going for a B.F.A.—a Bachelor of Fine Arts—will be competing with other art students primarily on the basis of their portfolios. Grades for B.F.A. applicants do matter too, simply because poor grades indicate a higher danger for dropping out, no matter how good an artist the student may be. All art students are strongly recommended to attend one or more portfolio day programs in regional locations, where groups of admission officers from art schools nationwide come together to give students feedback on their work. The National Portfolio Day Association (www.npda.org) sponsors them in more than thirty cities throughout the country, and more are organized under local aegis. In addition to the work itself, the art of taking slides, photographs, or a video is also crucial because portfolios are generally delivered in those media. Each institution offers specifications for portfolio submission, which should be followed to the letter.

> When you visit a college, leave a note for your local rep to let them know you visited.
>
> —Counselor's heads-up

DECEMBER 3–9, 2006

The second week of December is not pretty. Most seniors are staring down the barrel of semester exams and the final sprint to finish January applications. Many are also in suspended animation waiting for the results from the early round, which probably won't come until next week.

The final week before winter break is always a madhouse, so this is the time for students to politely check with teachers and counselors to make sure that recommendations and transcripts have been sent or will be sent. If applying for financial aid, get the paper version of the Free Application for Federal Student Aid (FAFSA) from the guidance office. If you plan to apply online—the quickest option that cuts down on errors—go to www.pin.ed.gov to get a PIN for you and one parent. Where applicable, register to receive the CSS/PROFILE via a paper form available in the high school guidance office or at www.collegeboard.com.

Eleventh graders will be happy to know that College Board mails PSAT results from the October test this week. The **American Fire Sprinkler Association Essay Contest** is a well-known if esoteric competition with seven one-time scholarships of up to $4,000. The **NASSP Principal's Leadership Award** competition takes place each fall in selected high schools, and high schools must choose their winner by early December to compete for 150 one-time scholarships of $1,000. The **National Academy of Television Arts and Sciences** offers two renewable scholarships of $10,000 per year to students who plan to major in a TV-related field.

Sunday, December 3

☐ PSAT results mailed to schools this week

_____

_____

Monday, December 4

_____

_____

_____

Tuesday, December 5

- [ ] American Fire Sprinkler Association Essay Contest. www.afsascholarship.org
- [ ] NASSP Principal's Leadership Award. www.principals.org

- [ ] Oglethorpe College, scholarship deadline
- [ ] Presbyterian College, early-decision and scholarship deadline

Wednesday, December 6

Thursday, December 7

Friday, December 8

- [ ] National Academy of Television Arts and Sciences Scholarship Deadline. www.emmyonline.org

Saturday, December 9

- [ ] ACT administered

DECEMBER 10–16, 2005

There is no use sugarcoating the week of December 15. Some kids will be winners and some will be losers as they log on to learn the fate of their early applications. (A few still wait for a decision letter in the mail.) Anyone with a heart hates this week.

Regular-admission deadlines arrive at **University of Minnesota–Twin Cities** and **Stanford. Connecticut College** and **Middlebury** have implemented a sneaky part I application deadline that requires students to submit a check and information sheet in advance of the final deadline. Early-decision deadlines include **Holy Cross, Rochester Institute of Technology,** and **Susquehanna,** among others. Early-action deadlines include **Beloit, Hampshire, Ohio Wesleyan,** and **Wabash.** A number of institutions have scholarship deadlines, including **Kenyon, Redlands, Tulane** and **Washington & Lee.** (See the appendices for complete lists.)

The **National Beta Club** offers more than two hundred one-time scholarships of up to $15,000 to students who are members of Beta Club, which has 7,500 chapters in forty-one states and emphasizes service and leadership. The **AXA Achievement Scholarship** program, administered in association with *U.S. News & World Report*, offers ten awards of $25,000 and forty-two awards of $10,000 to students throughout the nation who have shown outstanding achievement in a nonacademic project. The **Burger King Scholars** program offers 1,500 one-time awards to twelfth graders who must work at least fifteen hours per week and have financial need. One student is nominated per school. The **Hispanic Scholarship Fund** offers awards of up to $2,500 through its National High School Scholarship program. Other programs administered by the fund have various deadlines.

Sunday, December 10

☐ National Beta Club Scholarship. www.betaclub.org

☐ University of Southern California, scholarship deadline

Monday, December 11

_____

_____

_____

Wednesday, December 13

Thursday, December 14

Friday, December 15

- ☐ Regular-admission deadlines
- ☐ Early-decision and early-action deadlines
- ☐ Middlebury and Connecticut College, part I deadline
- ☐ Institutional-scholarship deadlines
- ☐ AXA Achievement Scholarship Deadline
  www.axa-achievement.com

- ☐ Burger King Scholars Program.
  www.bk.com
- ☐ Hispanic Scholarship Fund.
  www.hsf.net/scholarships.php

Saturday, December 16

SENDING EXTRA MATERIAL

Along with the stress of completing applications, many applicants wonder if they should top off their applications with something more. Some pieces of art? A musical tape? An article from the school newspaper?

Sending extra material can be a good move, or it can be a disaster. Here are some guidelines:

- **Ask first.** If you have previously met with a college representative from a particular school, an emailed question about extra material would be a good way to keep the conversation going. Find out the guidelines for extra material. Some colleges toss out anything that does not fit in a 9" x 12" folder. Others farm the material out to a relevant academic department.

- **Do it in moderation.** You won't be needing that middle school science project that Aunt Emma thought was so special. Students should limit themselves to the one or two most impressive items, preferably produced in the past year. Choosing between similar items is sometimes hard but a better strategy than sending everything.

- **Make it good.** Realize that material in visual arts, performing arts, and journalism (to name a few) may find its way to an evaluator who is a faculty member in the field. Just because you have the nicest alto voice in the school choir does not mean that you will stand out in the context of national competition.

We know at least one admission office that has an end-of-the-year party where the entertainment is all the lousy tapes and videos that students have sent in. Most students who get into most colleges send only the application. Make sure that the rationale behind extra material is compelling.

HANDLING AN EARLY DEFERRAL OR DENIAL

It hurts when you don't get in early. Denials in March or April come paired with acceptances. In December, one decision is all that comes.

You know this is not the end of the world, but give yourself time to grieve. Parents, empathize but don't show too much disappointment yourself. Pep talks won't mean as much as modeling a balanced, realistic approach. This one did not work out, but others will. Colleges make decisions in the context of a particular group that applies for admission in a particular year. Every college and every year are different. There is an element of randomness anyway. Small consolation.

As soon as possible, students should set their sights on the work ahead—more applications.

Many students will not be denied outright, but will instead be deferred. Alas, the odds of deferred students getting in are generally low—significantly lower than the overall acceptance rate. Students with their heart set on a particular school can express continuing interest and update the college on new activities, similar to a wait-list situation. (See page 214.) But the realistic approach is generally to move on.

> I participated in a Colgate online chat and it was the most useful thing I did. I was given the opportunity to talk with faculty, current students, and other accepted students.
>
> —Colgate University student

DECEMBER 2006

TOP FIVE MYTHS OF COLLEGE ADMISSION

5. That students with straight As and high SAT scores should get in anywhere. The sobering truth is that just because you stand out at your school doesn't mean you'll stand out in the applicant pool of an Ivy. If you get 700's and have a 3.8 GPA, that makes you an average applicant at Dartmouth or Stanford. Being average puts your odds at 20 percent or less, and that's before considering that most admitted students have a special talent or ability that puts them over the top.

4. That getting in is about strategy. Playing your cards right can help a little, but we're talking maybe 5 percent of the getting-in equation. Most college credentials can't be manufactured, and admission officers can see through the attempts of students (and their parents) to try to jazz up an unexciting applicant.

3. That getting in is about pulling strings. If only admission officers had a nickel for every applicant whose mother has a friend whose uncle is on the board of trustees. Don't be deluded by the idea that your close family friend can peddle influence. Unless your granddad gave the school a million dollars, you're better off applying on your own merit.

2. That college admission is a crap shoot. Admission decisions can seem random because high school students don't see the big picture. The goal of every college is to assemble a diverse and interesting class, and everybody who is admitted fills a role. The odds of admission at a particular school can change from year to year because both the pool of applicants and the college's needs change from year to year.

1. That the college admission process is fair. Life isn't fair, either. Just because you are good enough does not mean that you'll get in. The good news? If you apply to a sensible list of colleges, your college search will be a success, even if you can't control what happens at any particular college.

WINTER BREAK DEADLINE EMERGENCY

It is every counselor's nightmare to get a phone call on Christmas Eve from a stressed-out applicant. It happens. Maybe you were deferred in the early round. Maybe, after thinking about it, you have decided to apply to just one more school—and it happens to have a January 1 deadline. Remain calm. Do not call 911 or pull the fire alarm. The student should call the office first, then home—and be very, very nice about it. Most counselors are prepared to come in during the break to take care of odds and ends. Some may even be at school. Don't sweat it if you can't get in touch with the counselor. As long as your part of the application is sent by the deadline, the school's part(s) can come a few days later.

WHAT'S IN A DEADLINE?

As you're racing toward the post office on December 31, it may be comforting to know that most college deadlines are for postmark rather than receipt. With thousands upon thousands of pieces coming in at the deadline, it may take them several weeks to simply open the mail (one reason electronic filers can get their applications completed quicker). That doesn't mean it pays to wait until the last minute. A date of receipt is noted on everything that comes into the admission office. They know who procrastinated and who didn't. The odds of such a thing making a difference in any particular case are low, but colleges are aware that the students who get their applications completed early tend to be on-the-ball, go-getter types. Applications that are completed early get the first read, and they may be read more thoroughly than ones that squeak in at the last minute. This is nothing you can put your finger on—but food for thought.

And remember: Many deadlines for independent scholarships are for receipt, not postmark, and scholarship committees will not hesitate to disqualify applications who are even one day late.

DECEMBER 17–23, 2005

Ah, the blessed relief of winter break. With the fall semester now in the rearview mirror, the toughest grind is over. A few students may yet be staring at exams in January—not a pleasant thought. Many will use the winter break to finish off applications. There will be some procrastinators in the bunch, but for harried superachievers who run in ten different directions during the school year, the winter break can be a much-needed block of time.

The January SAT date is still available. Colleges with deadlines in January prefer the December date, but scores from January will get there in time. For students who took a December Subject Test and bombed it, January might give them another shot.

Sunday, December 17

Monday, December 18

Tuesday, December 19

Wednesday, December 20

_____   _____

_____   _____

_____   _____

Thursday, December 21

☐ January SAT and Subject Tests, registration deadline   _____
(approximate)
                                         _____

_____   _____

Friday, December 22

_____   _____

_____   _____

_____   _____

Saturday, December 23

_____   _____

_____   _____

_____   _____

DECEMBER 24–31, 2006

Whose bright idea was it to make all the application deadlines at the end of the holiday season? So much for family bonding. Maybe you'll get some quality time in the car on the way to the 24–7 post office.

The **Sons of the American Revolution Knight Essay Contest** offers three one-time awards of up to $7,500 to students in grades eleven and twelve based on an essay about the American Revolution. Essays must be submitted locally, and though deadlines vary by state, most are December 31. Visit the SAR website to find the contact in your state. The last day to request an application in the **Mensa Education and Research Foundation**'s essay contest is December 31, with submissions due January 15. The essay, not to exceed 550 words, should explain the student's academic and vocational goals and how they plan to achieve them. More than one hundred one-time scholarships of up to $4,000 are available. Students must live in the area of a participating Mensa group.

Sunday, December 24

Monday, December 25

Tuesday, December 26

Wednesday, December 27

Thursday, December 28

Friday, December 29

Saturday, December 30

Sunday, December 31

☐ Clemson University scholarship deadline

☐ Mensa MERF Essay Contest.
www.merf.us.mensa.org/scholarships/index.php

☐ Sons of American Revolution Knight Essay Contest.
www.sar.org

JANUARY 2007

FOR TWELFTH GRADERS WHO HAVE DONE THEIR HOMEWORK, January will be a snap. Students can put the finishing touches on January 15 applications and add one or two more schools if they are so moved. Financial aid applications should be filed by the end of the month. Students who have been knee-deep in the admission process can use this month to refocus on the scholarship search.

Eleventh graders should begin the college search in earnest this month and plan for spring break visits. Now is also the time to think about a standardized test schedule for the spring. What combination of SAT, ACT, and the Subject Tests should you take? See page 49 and page 83. January is also a good time to give serious thought to summer and make advance arrangements when necessary.

WHAT TO DO:

✓ **Monday, January 1**
Regular-decision deadlines at the most selective colleges

✓ **Friday, January 5**
February ACT, registration deadline

✓ **Monday, January 15**
Regular-decision deadlines at highly selective colleges

✓ **Saturday, January 27**
SAT and Subject Tests administered

JANUARY 1–6, 2007

The end of the application push is in sight for the Class of 2007. January 1 is the admission deadline at heavy-hitter national institutions, including the **Ivy League, MIT, Caltech, Duke**, and **Northwestern**. Binding Early Decision II deadlines include **Bates, Davidson, Emory, Hobart and William Smith, Swarthmore**, and **Washington U. (MO)**. (For a complete list of January 1 deadlines, see Appendix B.)

January 1 is also the first day that the FAFSA can be filed for students entering college in the fall of 2007. Families should do everything possible to secure W-2's and 1099's in a timely way.

Members of the Class of 2008 may seem like mere babes, but it is time for them to get serious about college admission tests if they have not already done so. Families should make a testing plan for the spring, which may or may not include the February ACT, which has its registration deadline this week.

Monday, January 1

☐ Application deadlines at the most selective colleges

☐ Round II early decision deadline

☐ Institutional-scholarship deadlines

☐ First day to file the 2007–2008 Free Application for Federal Student Aid (FAFSA)

Tuesday, January 2

Wednesday, January 3

☐ January SAT and Subject Tests, late-registration deadline (approximate)

Thursday, January 4

Friday, January 5

☐ February ACT, registration deadline

Saturday, January 6

January 7–13, 2006

The January 10 deadline list for regular decision includes **Cooper Union** (art only), **Elon, Georgetown, Occidental, Rice**, and **University of Southern California**.

All but a few procrastinators in the Class of 2006 should be finished with their applications by this date. As students slide into the laid-back mode of second-semester seniors, now would be a good time to focus again on the scholarship search.

Run by the John F. Kennedy Presidential Library, the **JFK essay contest** offers one-time scholarships up to $3,000 for students in grades 9–12. The **Ron Brown Scholar Program** is the nation's most competitive for African Americans. In a recent year, 8,500 students applied for the twenty scholarships totaling $40,000 for four years. The **Discover Card Tribute Award** is among the nation's premier recognition programs for eleventh graders, with nearly five hundred one-time awards of up to $25,000. The **Elks MVS** offers five hundred renewable awards of up to $15,000 per year, and financial need is a factor. The **United Nations Association National High School Essay Contest**, open to students in grades nine through twelve, offers three one-time awards of up $1,000. The **Telluride Association** sponsors two of the nation's elite summer programs in the humanities—one open to all and one for African American students. Both are free.

Sunday, January 7

☐ Villanova University, admission deadline

☐ JFK Profile in Courage Essay Contest.
www.jfkcontest.org

Monday, January 8

☐ Ron Brown Scholar Program Deadline.
www.ronbrown.org

Tuesday, January 9

Wednesday, January 10

- ☐ Regular admission deadlines at Cooper Union (art only), Elon, Georgetown, Occidental, Rice, and USC.
- ☐ Discover Card Tribute Award. www.discovercard.com/tribute.htm

- ☐ Telluride Association Summer Programs, approximate deadline. www.tellurideassociation.org

Thursday, January 11

Friday, January 12

- ☐ Elks Most Valuable Student Scholarship. www.elks.org/enf/scholars/mvs.cfm

- ☐ United Nations Association National High School Essay Contest. www.unausa.org

Saturday, January 13

"Your Application Is Incomplete"

They strike like a thunderbolt in the night: Computer-generated letters and emails bearing an ominous warning that transcripts or recommendations are missing. Wasn't the school supposed to have sent that material weeks ago? At 7:00 the next morning, Mom is on the phone with the college counseling office to find out what went wrong.

Usually, there is no problem. Colleges take a better-safe-than-sorry approach to sending these letters, often after the material in question has already been received. Here's an example. Suppose Alice is applying to Most Prestigious U. Her counselor, a virtuous soul, is working during the winter break and sends Alice's transcript on December 28. It arrives at MPU on January 3, is opened on January 6, and is entered into its computer system on January 12 (a relatively speedy timeline for January). Meanwhile, Alice applies using the online application on January 5. Two days later, MPU's computer notes that it has received Alice's application but not her transcript. On January 11, a letter is generated to Alice with the message that her transcript has not been received. The letter is mailed to Alice on January 14 and received on January 17, putting the family in panic city.

This is just one scenario. Many applicants get missing-credential letters. They are a routine part of the admission process, though each should be followed up on and resolved. Occasionally, material has been lost (by the college) or not sent, and there is almost never a problem with simply resending it.

> Be prepared to rewrite and revise your essay multiple times. I think I did mine about six.
>
> —Yale University student

Even when you know everything has been sent, it makes sense to keep following up until the colleges confirm receipt. Most schools allow students to check the status of their applications online—including updates on which items of the application have and have not been logged into the their computer.

WILL I BE COMPETING AGAINST OTHERS AT MY SCHOOL?

High school students eye each other nervously when they are interested in the same college. Since their schoolmates are the only ones they know who are also applying to "their" college, students naturally reduce the admission game to a head-to-head competition with Johnny Genius who sits in the front row in AP English.

It isn't necessarily so. Colleges do read applications by high school, but they almost never have quotas for particular ones. In one year, three students may get in from the same school; the next year, no one may get in. If one student is a math whiz and the other is a linebacker, they are more likely to compete with other math whizzes and linebackers than against each other. The same goes if one is the daughter of an alumnus and the other is a minority student.

Sometimes competition among students at the same school does play a role. If four students apply to Pomona one year, and the next year twelve apply, it may be harder to get in at Pomona for that particular year. But situations like that are relatively rare. With thousands of students in the applicant pool, a student's odds of admission are likely to be the same whether or not Johnny Genius happens to apply.

> We helped our daughter make a weekly to-do list in October of twelfth grade when it was clear that deadlines were coming fast and furious.
>
> —Washington University in St. Louis mom

JANUARY 14–20, 2007

The list of January 15 admission deadlines includes **Colorado College, Emory, George Washington** (part II), **Oberlin, Reed**, and **Trinity (CT)**. Institutions with Early Decision II deadlines include **Colgate, Franklin & Marshall, Hartwick, Skidmore**, and **Wheaton (MA)**. (See Appendix B for a complete list of January 15 deadlines.)

The nation's leading scholarship for minority students—the **Gates Millennium**—offers more than one thousand renewable full-ride scholarships with financial need as a factor. The **Phi Delta Kappa** scholarship offers one-time scholarships up to $5,000 to prospective education majors. The **Department of Agriculture 1890 scholarship** offers renewable full-boat awards to students looking at historically black colleges, and the **Young Naturalist Awards** program gives prizes up to $2,500 for outstanding science projects in biology, earth science, or astronomy. YNA is sponsored by the American Museum of Natural History. Students in grades seven through twelve may enter. The **DuPont Challenge**, open to students in grades seven through twelve, requires an essay of not more than one thousand words on a scientific topic for one-time scholarships up to

Sunday, January 14

Monday, January 15

- ☐ Application deadlines at highly selective colleges
- ☐ Early Decision II deadlines at moderately selective colleges
- ☐ Gates Millennium Scholarship. www.gmsp.org
- ☐ Phi Delta Kappa International Scholarship. www.pdkintl.org/studser/sschol.htm

- ☐ USDA 1890 National Scholars. 1890scholars.program.usda.gov
- ☐ Young Naturalist Awards. www.amnh.org/nationalcenter/youngnaturalistawards

Tuesday, January 16

_____   _____

_____   _____

Wednesday, January 17

☐ The DuPont Challenge Essay Contest.
  www.glcomm.com/dupont   _____

                                 _____

Thursday, January 18

_____   _____

_____   _____

Friday, January 19

☐ February ACT, late-registration deadline   ☐ National Honor Society Scholarship.
☐ Grinnell College, admission deadline   www.nhs.us

_____   _____

Saturday, January 20

_____   _____

_____   _____

JANUARY 21–27, 2007

Members of the Class of 2007 should take advantage of the January lull to refocus on the scholarship search. Some deadlines have passed, but there are still plenty in February through April. This is especially true of local awards, which tend to have later deadlines. (See page 192.) The January SAT is absolutely, positively the last one that can be used for admission to selective colleges. Seniors should use this date only in a pinch—to retake a test that they messed up on the first time, or to make one final attempt at increasing a score that is too low for their liking.

Sunday, January 21

Monday, January 22

Tuesday, January 23

Wednesday, January 24

_____

_____

_____

Thursday, January 25

_____

_____

_____

Friday, January 26

_____

_____

_____

Saturday, January 27

☐ SAT and Subject Tests administered

_____

_____

JANUARY 28–31, 2007

FAFSA and CSS/PROFILE filers should scramble to meet the February 1 deadline of most highly selective colleges. File on the basis of completed tax forms if possible, but don't miss a deadline waiting for a stray W-2.

Some parents may note that the FAFSA only allows families to send reports to six colleges—a bummer that has irritated families for years. Parents should file the form with the student's six first-choice schools. Then a) when the student aid report (SAR) comes back, send a copy of it to the remaining colleges; or b) make a "correction" on the SAR by erasing some of the initial list and substituting the schools previously omitted. The latter strategy works because the FAFSA processor has already sent reports to the first list. However, this method won't work if you must make other corrections to the SAR, since any schools you cross out now will not get the amended report.

For this week's lone scholarship deadline, **Papa John's Pizza** offers more than one thousand one-time scholarships nationwide of $1,000 to students who live in their delivery areas. **Navy ROTC** offers renewable full tuition and books at approximately 150 participating universities in exchange for a commitment to serve after graduation.

Sunday, January 28

_____

_____

Monday, January 29

_____

_____

Tuesday, January 30

_____

_____

_____

Wednesday, January 31

☐ University of Miami (OH), application deadline

☐ Navy ROTC Deadline. www.todaysmilitary.com

☐ Papa John's Scholars. www.papajohnsscholars.com

THE PRESIDENTIAL SCHOLARS PROGRAM

Each year, in the month of January, about 2,600 seniors with stratospheric test scores will be invited to apply for the Presidential Scholars Program. Of these, about 120 will be chosen for an all-expenses-paid week in Washington to meet with public officials and attend cultural events. All Presidential Scholars receive a medallion courtesy of the White House.

SCHOLARSHIPS FOR LEFT-HANDED STUDENTS?

The come-ons are everywhere: "Billions in unclaimed aid." "Free seminar tells all." "Act now." Few facets of American life have been so thoroughly scammed as the scholarship search.

The old chestnut about scholarships for left-handed students is typical—a misleading myth with just enough truth so that isn't an outright lie. This one was perpetuated for years by a popular scholarship guide, and by talk-show producers chasing an oddball story. It turns out that the scholarship for left-handed students is an institutional award at tiny Juniata College. It is available only to returning students and only to those who show financial need. Maximum amount: $1,500.

More ominous are the pitches that come in the mail for seminars in which the secrets of free money for college will presumably be revealed.

Typically, these outfits rent space in a local hotel or conference facility. They start out talking about money for college and end up with a sales pitch for financial services that you don't want to buy. The Federal Trade Commission has attempted to nail some of these organizations, which typically skirt truth-in-advertising laws. Learn more about scholarship scams at www.ftc.gov.

Smart families never pay anything for scholarship search services. The best scholarship search vehicle on the Web, www.fastweb.com, is free.

Another rule to keep in mind: Nearly 95 percent of all money for college comes via the institution where the student enrolls (including most federal aid). For anyone trying to find a scholarship, the first places to look are the colleges where the student will apply.

How Admission Offices Really Work

Few things are more shrouded in mystery than what admission officers do behind closed doors. The reality isn't particularly glamorous and can be summarized in three words: read, read, read.

> We talked to our daughter about why she procrastinated. Sometimes, there was stuff she was afraid to do. We tried to help her find good ways to approach these things.
>
> —Stanford University mom

Once an application is complete, it goes to a first reader, generally the regional representative who visited the high school in the fall. Admission officers (AOs) have a quota of applications they must evaluate every day that runs into the dozens, making for a lot of late nights in February and March. In about ten minutes, a seasoned AO can read the application, essays, transcripts, recommendations, and anything else that may be part of a file. The AO generally gives each file a rating—often two or more ratings for academic and personal qualities. High ratings mean admit and low ones mean deny. Typically, the file is then passed to a second reader. If the second reader agrees with the ratings of the first, and if those ratings point to clear admission or denial, the file will be processed or sent to the dean for approval of the decision. People such as coaches and alumni directors also have a major say in the process; any student who is on their short list has a big advantage.

Borderline applicants are fought over in committee, with each regional representative making the case for those from his or her area. This is when it can get ugly. At the most competitive schools, AOs often have to go back and cut out applicants who were initially on the admit list to get the class down to size. The full committee, generally including all the admission officers plus some faculty readers, will have representatives from all corners of the college who will go toe-to-toe for applicants who strike a chord with them.

One of the biggest myths is that admission offices are looking for well-rounded applicants. There is nothing wrong with being well-rounded, but the most compelling candidates generally have one or two passions that can contribute to a well-rounded class. For a complete overview of how colleges choose applicants, see the *Fiske Guide to Getting into the Right College*.

FEBRUARY 2007

SENIORS SHOULD FOLLOW UP ON APPLICATIONS via the Internet to make sure they are complete. Most financial aid deadlines are this month. Financial aid filers should watch for correspondence through the mail (paper filers) or online (electronic filers). Verify that information is correct. Families with special financial circumstances should contact the colleges directly. (See page 185.) Juniors should continue researching colleges and meet with college counselors where possible. Register for the March SAT and/or the April ACT where applicable. Families should solidify plans for college visits during spring break and continue weighing summer options.

WHAT TO DO:

✓ **Thursday, February 1**
Application and financial aid deadlines at moderately selective colleges

✓ **Friday, February 2**
March SAT, registration deadline*

✓ **Saturday, February 10**
ACT administered

✓ **Thursday, February 15**
Application and financial aid deadlines at moderately selective colleges

*Approximate deadline. Check with www.collegeboard.com.

FEBRUARY 1–3, 2007

February 1 is deadline day at many moderately selective private colleges (and some very selective public ones) including **Franklin & Marshall, Rhodes, University of San Francisco, University of Texas at Austin, University of Wisconsin at Madison,** and **Wofford.** (For a complete list, see the appendices.) February 1 is also deadline day for financial aid applications at highly selective institutions.

For raw numbers of scholarships, the **Sam Walton** (of Wal-Mart fame) is probably the nation's largest, offering more than six thousand one-time awards of $1,000. **The Jaycees,** the Junior Chamber of Commerce, offers twenty-five one-time scholarships of $1,000, with leadership and financial need among the criteria. **Junior Achievement,** an organization that promotes business and economic literacy in schools, awards a range of scholarships with February 1 deadlines. The DAR, **Daughters of the American Revolution,** also offers a range of scholarships related to U.S. history, government, economics, historic preservation, and health professions. **Toshiba** teams up with the **National Science Teachers Association** to offer a contest for kids of all ages who work in teams to design a "technology of the future" for one-time awards of up to $10,000. The **U.S. Institute of Peace** essay contest is one of the best known of its kind, with more than fifty one-time scholarships of up to $10,000.

Deadlines at two selective summer programs run by MIT also come this week. The **Research Science Institute** is a small, elite program that attracts some of the nation's top technically oriented students. Best of all, the program is free. The **Women's Technology Program** is a magnet for the nation's top female students and a bargain at $1,000 for six weeks. Both RSI and WTP are for students who have completed eleventh grade. (See Summer for Free, page 90.)

Thursday, February 1

- [ ] Application deadlines at moderately selective colleges
- [ ] Financial aid application deadlines at highly selective private colleges
- [ ] Announcement of National Merit Finalists
- [ ] Jaycee War Memorial Fund Scholarship. www.usjaycees.org/scholarships.htm
- [ ] Sam Walton Community Scholarship. www.walmartfoundation.org

- [ ] Junior Achievement Scholarships. www.ja.org
- [ ] DAR Scholarships. www.dar.org
- [ ] Toshiba/NSTA ExploraVision Awards. www.exploravision.org
- [ ] National Peace Essay Contest. www.usip.org/ed/npec/index.html
- [ ] MIT Research Science Institute. www.mit.edu
- [ ] Women's Technology Program. www.mit.edu

Friday, February 2

- [ ] March SAT, registration deadline

Saturday, February 3

FEBRUARY 4–10, 2007

This week includes the deadline for a third of MIT's high-powered summer programs for students who have completed eleventh grade. The **Minority Introduction to Engineering, Entrepreneurship, and Science** is a tuition-free, six-week program for minority students and disadvantaged non-minorities. (See Summer for Free, page 90.) The **Horace Mann Scholarship**, the nation's premier program for children of teachers and other school employees, offers twenty-six one-time scholarships of up to $10,000.

Sunday, February 4

Monday, February 5

☐ MIT Minority Introduction to Engineering, Entrepreneurship, and Science Summer Program. web.mit.edu/mites/www

Tuesday, February 6

Wednesday, February 7

Thursday, February 8

Friday, February 9

Saturday, February 10

☐ ACT administered

☐ Horace Mann Student Scholarship Program.
www.horacemann.com

Is There a Prep School Advantage?

The psychology of college admission plays interesting tricks. Just ask a student or parent from an elite boarding school how the process works. They'll tell you that the deck is stacked against East Coast prep schools. Public school kids, they say, can get a 4.0 GPA with no sweat while students at prep schools must scratch and claw for a 3.0. And with more of the smart kids concentrated in places like Connecticut and Massachusetts, the competition is much tougher for them than for students in, say, Indiana.

On the other hand, a public school parent from the Heartland may be thoroughly convinced that students at fancy private schools have the inside track at Harvard or Yale. The nation's top prep schools can get ten or more students into places like those in a single year; the typical public school may not see a student admitted in ten years.

The truth lies somewhere in the middle. Colleges always say that they evaluate students in the context of their school. The colleges make it their business to know how grading patterns vary from place to place. East Coast residents do have a harder time getting into East Coast colleges—more because of the colleges' desire for geographic diversity than anything else. At the ultra-competitive colleges, it is true that the top student at a no-name high school in Arkansas has a better shot than students in the middle of the pack at Milton Academy or Exeter.

But students at top private schools and savvy suburban publics get better college counseling than their peers elsewhere. They know how to play the angles, such as early decision, and counselors at high falutin' schools do have a degree of pull when the chips are down. (see page 191.) Some colleges will admit a student simply because he or she is from a certain high school—hoping that more students will follow. Students from lesser-known schools also have more pressure on them when it comes to standardized tests. A transcript from a prominent high school speaks for itself, but students from remote schools may need high standardized test scores to confirm their A's.

Students from all backgrounds get into top colleges. But with applications rising and acceptance rates shrinking, more are also feeling the pain of rejection. To these students, the process rarely seems fair.

SURVIVING THE AUDITION

Students who think that an interview is scary ought to try their hand at an audition. The best high school performers in music and drama are old pros at producing under pressure, but the audition raises the stakes to a new level. Auditions are a one-shot deal in front of admission officers and faculty that make or break admission chances.

Scheduling is crucial for auditions, especially when students are applying to a number of institutions. Pay careful attention to how each college or conservatory spells out its guidelines. Some have dates or windows of time in which students are expected to come to campus. Others have regional auditions at off-campus locations. Coordinating these schedules and following up can be a headache, and admission offices for music and drama programs tend not to be as organized as those for, say, accounting. Stay on top of them and call to confirm your schedule.

The right choice of a piece(s) to act, play, or sing in the audition can be the most crucial ingredient of success. Applicants should make sure that they understand each college's guidelines and then consult with someone, such as a teacher or coach, who can give them expert advice.

FEBRUARY 11–17, 2007

Colleges and universities with February 15 application deadlines include private institutions such as **Gettysburg, Rollins, St. Lawrence University,** and **College of Wooster,** and public institutions such as **University of Arkansas** and **State University of New York at Stony Brook.** (See the appendices for a complete list.)

The **EF Global Citizen Essay Contest** offers twelve one-time scholarships of $1,000 and a ten-day trip to Europe. A school nomination is required. The **National Alliance for Scholastic Achievement** emphasizes

Sunday, February 11

Monday, February 12

Tuesday, February 13

Wednesday, February 14

☐ March SAT, late-registration deadline (approximate)

_____

_____

_____

_____

_____

Thursday, February 15

☐ Application deadlines at moderately selective colleges

☐ Financial aid deadlines at moderately selective private colleges and public universities

☐ EF Global Citizen Essay Contest. School nomination required. www.eftours.com

_____

Friday, February 16

☐ National Alliance for Scholastic Achievement Scholarship. www.eee.org/bus/nasa

_____

_____

_____

Saturday, February 17

_____

_____

_____

_____

_____

_____

FEBRUARY 18–24, 2007

Parents of twelfth-grade financial aid filers are advised to make sure that their applications are on track. By now, families should have received a copy of the FAFSA student aid report (SAR) and a similar document from the CSS/PROFILE, either electronically or through the mail. (Snail-mail filers be aware that the SAR will come addressed to the student.)

The **USA Today All-Academic Team** provides one-time awards of $2,500 to twenty students who are nominated by their schools. The April ACT date is the preferred spring alternative at many high schools, though some students decide to wait until June when school is out.

Sunday, February 18

Monday, February 19

Tuesday, February 20

☐ USA Today All-Academic Team.
School nomination required.
www.usatoday.com

Wednesday, February 21

Thursday, February 22

Friday, February 23

Saturday, February 24

RED FLAGS FROM THE ADMISSION OFFICE

Most admission officers treat their applicants with the utmost professionalism. Yet at least half of all AOs are in their early twenties, and intentionally or not, they do make mistakes. Here are a few common ones:

- **Saying test scores are no big deal.** Some admission officers have convinced themselves that standardized test scores don't matter. They're humanists, after all. But the fact is that test scores do matter—a lot. The transcript is the most important factor in admission, but among students who have strong transcripts, test scores play a significant role.

- **Encouraging unrealistic applicants.** One of an admission officer's main jobs is to generate applications, whether or not those applications are from admissible applicants. Students who don't have a prayer of getting in can still have "great" interviews. For a reality check, head to your college counselor.

- **Asking students to name their first choice.** It is natural for admission officers to be curious about how their school rates on the student's priority list. But AOs are going too far if they press students to name all their college choices and/or which one is the top choice. Students should politely demur.

- **Encouraging early decision.** Admission officers may note that students have a better chance of admission if they apply early, but they should not cross the line of urging students to apply ED. The idea to apply ED should come from the student's head and nowhere else.

- **Pressing for a commitment.** According to the National Association for College Admission Counseling (NACAC), students should have until May 1 to make up their minds about where to go without financial penalty (unless they applied ED). Some colleges try to force students into a commitment before that date. If it happens to you, get the school counselor involved.

Most families can get a fair shake in the world of financial aid by filing the FAFSA, and where necessary, the CSS/PROFILE and/or the college's own financial aid form. (The PROFILE has additional supplements for non-custodial parents and those who are self-employed.) But some families have circumstances that beg further explanation. In such cases, there is no substitute for making your case to each aid office with a one- to two-page letter and supporting documentation. Among the usual scenarios:

- **An expected decline in earnings.** If your income was more last year than it will be this year, explain why. Include pay stubs if relevant. Be aware that if your income projection for the current year turns out to be low, the aid office will remember that when making its award the following year.

- **Unusual expenses.** If you're caring for Mom's father, or have health problems yourself that have recently cropped up, spell them out. Credit-card debt doesn't count.

- **Self-employment.** For good or ill, financial aid officers tend to view self-employed people with a skeptical eye, particularly if you have high revenue and high write-offs. If you're not making as much money as your cash flow would indicate, explain why.

- **Uncooperative non-custodial parent.** Many a student loses out in the aid process because the non-custodial parent won't help. Some aid offices will give you the benefit of the doubt if the divorce was a long time ago and the non-custodial parent has no role in the student's life.

> I had a student who was given a significantly better aid package from Harvard than from Princeton. Since his first choice was Princeton, I faxed his Harvard package to the Princeton financial aid people and they quickly matched the Harvard offer.
>
> —Counselor's heads-up

FEBRUARY 25–28, 2007

With the third quarter coming to a close in most schools, now is a good time for students to put their noses to the grindstone. We're not talking so much to the juniors, who may already have a nervous eye on upcoming AP tests. It is the Class of 2007 that we're worried about, those erstwhile super-achievers who have been magically transformed into slackers by second-semester senioritis. They'll deny it up and down—but we know better.

A little easing up is not a bad thing. The students who fall into a coma are the ones we are worried about. Colleges have been known to rescind offers of admission to kids who do a big-time nosedive. B's and even an occasional C on the final transcript are unlikely to cause a problem, but students who get several C's or a D will have some explaining to do. Two D's or an F could spell serious trouble. Why risk it? Third-quarter grades don't go to the colleges (except in wait-list situations) so anyone who is at risk still has time to pull up their grades in the fourth quarter.

The **Optimist International Essay Contest**, open to students in grades 9–12, features one-time scholarships up to $5,000. Check with local Optimist Clubs for deadlines. For the Class of 2008, the **Girls' Leadership Workshop** offers nine days of programming at Val-Kill, the one-time rural getaway cottage of Eleanor Roosevelt, who is the inspiration for the program. The registration fee is only $200.

Sunday, February 25

_____

_____

_____

Monday, February 26

_____

_____

_____

_____

_____

_____

☐ Queens College (CAN), admission deadline

☐ Optimist International Essay Contest.
www.optimist.org/prog-essay.html

☐ Girls' Leadership Workshop at Val-Kill, application
deadline. www.ervk.org

"WINK LETTERS" BRIGHTEN FEBRUARY SPIRITS

In late February or early March, a few lucky students get an attitude adjustment from the colleges in the form of a "wink letter." These are friendly little notes to see how the students are doing and to say that, by the way, they're probably in. Nothing official, just a heads-up. A sample of the colleges that have sent such letters to top applicants in recent years includes Clark, Cornell, Dartmouth, Duke, Grinnell, and Smith. Colleges mail these as an attempt to get a foot in the door with students who will probably have other options when the acceptance letters are mailed. No one should be upset if they don't get such a letter from these or other institutions; many students will be admitted who don't get one. Those who do receive one have the satisfaction of knowing that they are now the ones being pursued.

> One family seeking more financial aid chose to fly out to the college (four-thousand-mile round trip) to plead their case. Two members of the family went out. The cost of the trip undercut the family's message of dire financial straits.
>
> —**Counselor's heads-up**

MARCH 2007

DECISION LETTERS FOR THE CLASS OF 2007 will come in at an accelerating pace as the month progresses. Families should scrutinize aid packages and make plans for final college visits in April.

Juniors should use spring break for college visits and/or to prepare for standardized tests. Students in AP courses should make sure they are registered to take the exam.

WHAT TO DO:

✓ **Thursday, March 1**
Admission and financial aid deadlines at moderately selective colleges

✓ **Friday, March 9**
April ACT, registration deadline

✓ **Saturday, March 10**
SAT administered

✓ **Thursday, March 15**
Admission and financial aid deadlines at moderately selective colleges

MARCH 1–3, 2007

Admission deadlines at moderately selective institutions continue this week, including **Austin College, Florida State, Hampden-Sydney, Lake Forest, Ohio Wesleyan**, and **Purdue**. (See the appendices for a complete list.)

Kaplan's "My Turn" Essay Contest gives entrants in grades nine through twelve a shot at seeing their work in *Newsweek*'s feature by the same name as well as one-time awards up to $5,000. The week's other essay contest, sponsored by the **American Foreign Service** and also open to grades nine through twelve, offers one-time awards up to $2,500. The **National Alliance for Scholastic Achievement** emphasizes academic excellence in parceling out its five one-time scholarships of up to $15,000. The **Pfizer Epilepsy Scholarship Award**, offering awards up to $3,000, is among the most prominent awards available to students with a particular medical condition. The **Donna Reed Performing Arts Scholarships** include ten one-time awards of up to $4,000 for students who excel in acting, vocal music, and musical theater.

Carleton College offers one of the nation's premier summer programs for minority students, the **Liberal Arts Experience**. The program is open to students between tenth and eleventh grade. The program is one week long and the college pays all expenses, including travel. (See Summer for Free, page 90.) March 1 is the preferred date for nominations, the first step in the application process.

Thursday, March 1

- ☐ Admission and financial aid deadlines at moderately selective private colleges and public universities
- ☐ Kaplan/Newsweek "My Turn" Essay Contest. www.kaptest.com/essay
- ☐ SAR Rumbaugh Oration Contest. www.sar.org

- ☐ American Foreign Service High School Essay Contest. www.afsa.org
- ☐ Pfizer Epilepsy Scholarship Award. www.epilepsy-scholarship.com
- ☐ Donna Reed Performing Arts Scholarships. www.donnareed.org

_____

_____

_____

_____

_____

_____

HOW COUNSELORS USE THEIR CONNECTIONS

Parents may not say so out loud, but many expect more from a college counselor than simply sending off the transcripts and offering a good piece of advice now and then. They want a counselor who, when the chips are down, can pull the right string and get a kid into college.

Does it happen in real life? Maybe once in a while, but not in the way that most people envision. Here are some ways that high school counselors and admission officers typically interact:

- **They go over the list of applicants**. When a high school sends more than two or three applicants to a particular private college, the college counselor and admission officer often talk. The AO may call with a tentative list of decisions to get the counselor's feedback.

- **They discuss concerns.** Sometimes people on either side of the desk will want to talk about a concern related to a particular student, such as a blip in grades or a health issue. Uncertainty about an item on the transcript is another common topic.

- **The counselor may lobby for a particular student.** Counselors do make these calls, but smart ones do so only when they can meaningfully add to what has been submitted on paper. For instance, a student who contributes more to the intellectual life of the school than is reflected in his grades might be the subject of an "extra push" call by the counselor.

Counselors know that they cannot overplay their hand and make every candidate look like the greatest thing since sliced bread. Veteran counselors do have relationships with top admission officers, greased by annual conferences they both attend. Counselors at big-name private high schools or major suburban publics have a degree of clout at colleges where they send large numbers of students. Yet these same counselors could tell you a sad story about how the admit rate for traditional feeder high schools has steadily declined at big-name colleges in the last twenty years.

For their part, colleges are not going to allow a counselor to pull the wool over their eyes. For years, Princeton famously refused to interact with high school counselors beyond official communications. (Relations have thawed with a new dean in charge.) A good counselor can help students make their case, but students are the only ones who can get themselves in.

> Some of the best essays are on ordinary topics. The student does not have to build houses in Guatemala, climb Mt. Fiji, or kick the winning goal in a soccer championship.
>
> —Counselor's heads-up

SEARCHING FOR SCHOLARSHIPS: THE LOCAL ANGLE

This book includes a listing of the most prominent national scholarships. Something from that list may work out, though all national scholarship programs are very competitive. For obvious reasons, students have better odds at awards offered in their local community or state. A search on www.fastweb.com may locate some of these, but there is no substitute for working with the guidance office to find local awards. These may be offered by neighborhood associations, civic groups, churches, doctors, dentists, car dealerships, TV stations, and anyone else who wants to lend a hand to young people while getting a bit of publicity. In larger metropolitan areas, a local foundation may produce a scholarship directory that will list many of these awards. Deadlines are often in the spring.

WHAT HAS GOTTEN INTO YOU? PARENTS WANT TO KNOW

This phrase is commonly heard from the mouths of bewildered moms and dads in the spring of twelfth grade. Call it senioritis, pre-separation conflict, or the I'm-scared-to-leave-home blues. In its most acute form, it leads to knockdown battles over everything from homework to curfew.

What's happening here? Psychologists tell us that one way people deal with impending separation is to provoke conflict. Often, the intensity of the fighting is directly proportional to the strength of the bond between parent and child. Some students become more rebellious, others more withdrawn. Parents tend to react in the former case by asserting more control, and in the latter case by pushing harder to communicate. Neither is likely to work.

Parents should not be undone by an escalation of conflict as graduation approaches. It is part of the territory. Don't frantically try to fix things—or think that you only have a few months! Accept the fact that your relationship may not be fully back to normal until son or daughter goes away and gets some much-needed perspective. As always, parents need to keep an even keel. Maintain reasonable limits while cutting them a little more slack as they approach the time of leave-taking.

> Apply to at least one rolling admission school so you can get in somewhere quickly and feel good.
>
> —Arizona State student

MARCH 4–10, 2007

If you are currently enrolled in an AP course, you will probably be automatically registered to take the exam. The fee is about $82, with limited financial assistance available that may vary from school to school. Check with your school's AP coordinator. About 60 percent of the schools nationwide offer AP courses. If you would like to take an AP test but attend one of the 40 percent of schools that do not offer them, or if you are homeschooled, March 15 is the deadline for you to contact a school that does offer AP to make arrangements to take the tests. If considering this option, head to www.collegeboard.com for an overview of what each test covers, or buy a prep book from among the many available in bookstores. AP courses are generally a year long, so covering all the material will take some doing.

All-around academic and athletic excellence is the standard for the **Student Athlete Milk Mustache of the Year award**, which echoes the popular advertising campaign with the same theme. Twenty-five one-time scholarships of $7,500 are available. The **Tisch School of NYU** offers one of the nation's best arts-related summer programs, including courses in acting, dramatic writing, musical theater, and film.

Sunday, March 4

Monday, March 5

☐ Scholar Athlete Milk Mustache of the Year
(SAMMY) Award. www.whymilk.com

Tuesday, March 6

Wednesday, March 7

_____   _____
_____   _____
_____   _____

Thursday, March 8

_____   _____
_____   _____
_____   _____

Friday, March 9

☐ April ACT, registration deadline   _____
_____   _____
_____

Saturday, March 10

☐ Tisch Summer High School Programs, application   _____
   deadline. www.nyu.edu   _____
_____   _____

MARCH 11–17, 2007

The week's admission deadlines include **Clarkson, Muhlenberg, Ripon**, and **Stetson**. (See Appendix B for a complete list.) With spring break around the corner, now is the time for the Class of 2008 to follow through on making arrangements for any college visits.

U.S.A. Funds offers one-time scholarships up to $1,500 to minority students with financial need. The **Horace Mann Scholarship** offers twenty-six one-time scholarships of up to $10,000 for children of teachers and other school employees. The National Federation of Independent Business offers more than 300 scholarships of up to $10,000 through its **Free Enterprise Scholars Program** to students who have demonstrated entrepreneurial spirit.

Clark University's **Summer Science Program** is three weeks long and free for the taking for students who have completed eleventh grade. Among the nation's most unique summer programs is the **Freeman Asian Cultural Experience** in Sewanee, which offers participants a free two-week program for students who have completed tenth or eleventh grade. (See Summer for Free, page 90.)

Sunday, March 11

Monday, March 12

Tuesday, March 13

Wednesday, March 14

_____   _____

_____   _____

Thursday, March 15

- ☐ Admission deadlines at moderately selective colleges
- ☐ AP Exam registration deadline for homeschooled students and those at schools not offering AP
- ☐ Horace Mann Student Scholarship Program. www.horacemann.com

- ☐ U.S.A. Funds Access to Education Scholarship. www.usafunds.org
- ☐ NFIB Free Enterprise Scholars. www.nfib.com
- ☐ Clark University—Summer Science Program. www.clark.edu
- ☐ FACES Asian Studies Summer Program Deadline. www.sewanee.edu

Friday, March 16

_____   _____

_____   _____

Saturday, March 17

_____   _____

_____   _____

_____   _____

Regardless of why they took the year off or what they did, students could not be more effusive in their praise. Many talk of their year away as a "life-altering" experience or "turning point," and most feel that its full value can never be measured and will pay dividends the rest of their lives.

—Harvard University website

Count Harvard among those who recommend—emphatically—that students consider taking a year off between high school and college. A prime candidate is the student who is weary of the rat race—who studies hard but has forgotten why. Students considering a year off before college should complete the admission process with everyone else. Then, after the offers of admission come back, the student should write a letter to the first-choice college asking for a deferral of enrollment for one year. Most colleges will be happy to grant such a request with a reasonable outline of what the student plans to do. Students can always change their minds and go to a different college after the year off, but they will have the peace of mind that comes with a reserved spot in a class.

There are some potential glitches. Sometimes scholarships cannot be postponed a year, including some state-sponsored scholarships that are open to high school graduates. Without a concrete plan, a year off can be counterproductive, especially if the student becomes passive or takes a menial job that does not further personal growth.

Students considering a year off may want to consult one of the following:

- *The Back Door Guide to Short-Term Job Adventures: Internships, Extraordinary Experiences, Seasonal Jobs, Volunteering, Work Abroad,* by Michael Landes (Ten Speed Press)

- *Taking Time Off,* by Colin Hall and Ron Lieber (Princeton Review)

LIVING/LEARNING AND RESIDENTIAL COLLEGE PROGRAMS

Many high school students are star-struck at the thought of rubbing shoulders with the multitudes at a sprawling university. So much to do, so many new faces. They don't count on the fact that anonymity can breed alienation, and that falling asleep in the back of a five-hundred-seat lecture hall is not the recipe for a quality education.

Some major universities have a great invention for dealing with this problem: a residential college or living/learning unit. Such programs offer the benefits of a small community while retaining access to the vast resources beyond. The living/learning component comes in the form of, say, a lecture in the residence hall common room, or a trip to the symphony for everyone in the program, or maybe a seminar offered only to students in the living/learning hall. A number of private universities, including Yale, U of Miami, and Rice, to name three, divide the whole student body into residential colleges. The most famous living/learning program among public institutions is the University of Michigan's one-thousand-student Residential College. Other public institutions with residential colleges include UC–San Diego, UC–Santa Cruz, University of Illinois at Urbana-Champaign, UMass, UNC–Chapel Hill, and University of Wisconsin at Madison, to name a representative sample.

Conventional honors programs at state universities provide similar benefits, including small classes, access to top faculty, and enrichment programming. Living/learning and honors programs are two great ways to get a private college education at a state university price.

To really know what's going on at a college, talk to the maintenance staff and campus security. Go off the beaten path to look at buildings that were not included in the official tour.

—Counselor's heads-up

MARCH 18–24, 2007

With spring break at hand, the Class of 2007 has a perfect chance for some serious thinking about summer. Students should focus less on what they think will "look good" than on what they really want to do. Summer programs at colleges cost a king's ransom but provide a great taste of college life. Deadlines are typically in April or May. Summer work is perfectly honorable. So, too, is a shadowing experience or internship in a field of potential interest.

Sunday, March 18

Monday, March 19

Tuesday, March 20

Wednesday, March 21

_____   _____
_____   _____
_____   _____

Thursday, March 22

_____   _____
_____   _____
_____   _____

Friday, March 23

☐ April ACT, late-registration deadline   _____
_____   _____
_____   _____

Saturday, March 24

_____   _____
_____   _____
_____   _____

MARCH 25–31, 2007

For the Class of 2007, the **Young American Creative Patriotic Art** award features three one-time scholarships of $10,000 and is available to students in grades nine through twelve. Two Canadian universities, **University of British Columbia** and **Queen's University**, have application deadlines this week.

Also in the summer, **Landmark Volunteers** offers dozens of community service programs throughout the nation. The program is available to students who have completed grades nine through eleven and costs $875 in the form of a tax-deductible contribution for a two-week experience.

Sunday, March 25

_____   _____

_____   _____

Monday, March 26

_____   _____

_____   _____

Tuesday, March 27

_____   _____

_____   _____

Wednesday, March 28

Thursday, March 29

☐ Young American Creative Patriotic Art Award.
www.ladiesauxvfw.com

Friday, March 30

Saturday, March 31

☐ Landmark Volunteers Deposit Deadline.
www.volunteers.com

☐ University of British Columbia, Queen's University
(CAN) admission deadline

An Applicant's Worst Nightmare: Caught without a School

A denial from First Choice U is bad enough, but the worst case scenario in college admission is getting a thin letter from every school on the list. Such cases are rare, but they are happening more frequently in today's competitive climate.

If, God forbid, you get caught in this situation, there are a number of paths to consider:

- **Try again at the same schools.** This strategy has the best chance of success for students who are on the wait list. Your college counselor is probably best positioned to tell the sad story, which can increase the odds of admission if and when the wait list becomes active. (See page 214 for more on the wait list.)

- **Find new options.** Colleges don't like to say it too loudly, but plenty of them will consider strong applicants after April 1. A "spaces available" list circulates among high school counselors in late April, but even schools that are not on that list may find room. An acceptance can come within days.

- **Plan on a transfer.** A string of denials may indicate that the student's original college list was unrealistic. The student may choose to attend a community college or local state university with an eye toward transferring after a (one hopes) better academic performance next year.

- **Consider a postgraduate year.** Some boarding schools offer this option to students who have potential but need another year to mature. The environment tends to be structured and is no one's idea of fun, but students who do well may find their admission prospects drastically improved.

No one deserves the experience of having to scramble for a school in April. The good news is that for those who must do so, there are some reasonable options.

APRIL–JUNE 2007

SENIORS SHOULD WEIGH OFFERS, MAKE VISITS, and evaluate aid awards. Families can appeal low awards using a second, higher award as leverage. Wait-listed students should follow up promptly and vigorously. (See page 214.) Students wishing to take a year off before college should contact the colleges by phone and follow up with a letter. Students should reply to all offers of admission—including those they choose not to accept—by a postmark deadline of May 1.

The Class of 2008 should continue researching colleges with a goal of finding ten to twelve likely options by the end of school. Families should firm up summer plans and schedule college visits. Juniors applying to highly selective colleges should consider taking SAT Subject Tests in June.

WHAT TO DO:

✓ **Sunday, April 1**
Decisions at the most selective colleges mailed and available on the Web

✓ **Monday, April 12**
May SAT and Subject Tests, registration deadline*

✓ **Saturday, April 14**
ACT administered

✓ **Friday, May 4**
June ACT, registration deadline

✓ **Friday, April 27**
June SAT and Subject Tests, registration deadline*

✓ **Saturday, June 2**
SAT and Subject Tests administered

✓ **Saturday, June 9**
ACT administered

*Approximate deadline. Check with www.collegeboard.com.

APRIL 1–7, 2007

The nation's most selective colleges hand down their decisions on or about April 1. Drum roll, please. . . . As a parent, you should stay calm and above the fray. Reassure your student, repeatedly if necessary, that any college selection will offer great opportunities. If he or she has applied intelligently, you'll be telling the truth.

As for deadlines this week, the **Yoshiyama Award,** based solely on community service, requires a nomination and nets winners a one-time award of $5,000. One of the nation's biggest providers of scholarships for minority students, the **Jackie Robinson Foundation,** offers scholarships of up to $24,000 over four years for students with outstanding credentials who exceed 900 on the Critical Reading and Math portions of the SAT or 23 on the ACT. **CMU's Summer Academy for Minority Students** is a free, six-week program for rising eleventh and twelfth graders with an interest in science and math. (See Summer for Free, page

Sunday, April 1

☐ Decisions at highly selective colleges mailed or available on the Web

☐ University of Arizona, Eckerd College, Gustavus Adolphus College, Howard University, University of Iowa

☐ Yoshiyama Award. www.hitachi.org/yoshiyama

☐ Jackie Robinson Foundation Scholarship. www.jackierobinson.org

☐ Carnegie Mellon University—Summer Programs for Diversity. www.cmu.edu

Monday, April 2

☐ May SAT and Subject Tests, registration deadline (approximate)

Tuesday, April 3

Wednesday, April 4

_____   _____

_____   _____

_____   _____

Thursday, April 5

_____   _____

_____   _____

_____   _____

Friday, April 6

_____   _____

_____   _____

_____   _____

Saturday, April 7

_____   _____

_____   _____

_____   _____

THE NITTY GRITTY OF AID AWARDS

Only an accountant could enjoy the mind-numbing job of sifting through aid awards. The devil is in the details, so get out your magnifying glass. Your final decision probably won't depend on a thousand dollars here or there, but getting on top of the aid situation may help you pry more money from the college of choice. In the case of a toss-up, dollars may indeed make the difference. Here are some suggestions for evaluating aid awards:

- Be systematic. Need-based aid packages are a combination of grants (money you keep), loans (money you pay back), and work-study (the promise of government-subsidized employment to help pay the bills). The total amount of your aid package is less important than the amount of each component.

- Check the cost assumptions. If a college says it is meeting your full need, does it factor in an allowance for travel and living expenses? Some colleges consider these expenses in their awards; others do not, or do so with low-ball figures—which means the aid package won't cover the real bill.

- Consider PLUS loans radioactive. Some colleges don't meet the full financial need of applicants but want to look like they do. They pad their "aid" packages with market-rate PLUS loans that anyone can get, regardless of need. Look for loans that are "subsidized"—that means the government will pay the interest while the student is in school.

> I tried to make sure that my son had seen a variety of schools and understood what my opinion was and why it was my opinion. Then I let him choose.
>
> —University of Illinois at Urbana-Champaign dad

- Find out about next year. Is your merit scholarship renewable for four years? If so, the college should tell you the minimum GPA necessary to retain it. The usual is 3.0. Will the loan component of your package increase? The answer is probably yes—find out how much more in student loans will be expected during the upperclass years.

- Use better need-based offers as leverage. If the frontrunner college doesn't come through with the top financial aid offer, send a copy of the best offer to its aid office, along with a tactful request to review the calculations. Be sure to highlight special circumstances that other colleges may have considered more generously.

A few institutions, notably Williams College and Carnegie Mellon University, openly say that they will match other need-based offers in some circumstances. Many colleges will make an upward adjustment if you give them a rationale. (Merit awards, on the other hand, are usually firm.) Parents often do the heavy lifting with a financial aid appeal, but they should encourage their kids to take the lead when the students are comfortable doing so. A student's best ally is the admission officer who did the recruiting—call and see if the AO can help in dealing with the financial aid office.

Though thousands of dollars may be at stake, the issue of how the college deals with your appeal may be as important as the dollars involved. An offer of admission and aid is the beginning of a four-year relationship. The way you are treated now may be a barometer of how you will be treated later.

> I found that whenever I visited a school during cold or bad weather, I had less favorable impression of the school. My advice would be to try to block out influences like this.
>
> —Colby College student

In the throes of making a final decision, some students almost wish they had been accepted at only one school. After months of hoping, waiting, and wondering, students must now choose one place to go and send the equivalent of a rejection letter to the others. Add guilt to the roller coaster of emotions. Here are some pointers for making a good choice:

> Students should visit, eat the food, attend a class, and experience the school before paying the cash.
>
> —Counselor's heads-up

- **Consider visiting again.** Our recommendation is strongest for students whose first visit was in the summer. For any student, it is amazing how different a campus can look with a freshly mailed acceptance letter in hand.

- **Focus on the fit rather than the admission officer.** Students can develop strong attachments to AOs during the course of the process. This is not necessarily a bad thing, unless a great recruiter sells you the wrong college.

- **Make lists, clarify priorities.** Students are in a different place at the end of the process than they were at the beginning. You should reexamine your priorities, then compare and contrast the strengths of each choice based on those priorities.

- **Consult widely.** Students should compare notes with classmates, visit the guidance office, and call older friends who are already attending the colleges. They should even consider talking to Mom and Dad.

After all the analyzing—or even before—most students know in their heart where they want to go. Parents should use the advice above to help them uncover the truth that is already inside them.

SOME ACCEPTANCE LETTERS WE'D LIKE TO SEE
(TRANSLATED FOR PARENTS)

With the euphoria of acceptance still fresh for the Class of 2007, the grim reality for parents may now be sinking in:

"Congratulations! You've earned a place in the Class of 2011."
Congratulations! Your child has earned the right to pay us $150,000 of your money.

"The college has reviewed your credentials and is confident of your potential for success."
The college has reviewed your net worth and will leave you just enough money to maintain the lifestyle of a hunter–gatherer.

"In the weeks ahead, you'll receive an official welcome to the college community."
. . . it will include an official envelope in which to enclose your check. Payment is due in July.

APRIL 8–JUNE 15, 2007

The final weeks of high school are a whirlwind. After chomping at the bit for months and years, students tend to be taken aback by how fast the end comes. Take time to savor the moment.

For many students, the last act of serious school will be AP exams during the second and third weeks of May. Wait-listed students will probably learn their fate by mid-May, though occasionally the uncertainty can drag on into the summer. Here are a few last deadlines.

Scholarships and Contests

Sunday, April 15

☐ **AMVETS National Scholarship Deadline. (12) www.amvets.org**
The AMVETS scholarship offers six awards of $4,000 to veterans and their dependents.

Wednesday, April 25

☐ **The Ayn Rand Essay Contest. (12) www.aynrand.org/contests**
Sponsored by the foundation that carries on the work of the famed novelist/philosopher, this contest offers sixteen one-time awards between $1,000 and $10,000 for essays on The Fountainhead.

Monday, April 30

☐ **The Tylenol Scholarship Deadline. (12) scholarship.tylenol.com.**
The Tylenol Scholarship program is among the nation's largest, offering ten one-time scholarships of $10,000 and 150 scholarships of $1,000 to students who plan to major in health-related fields.

☐ **Holocaust Remembrance Essay Contest. (9–12) www.holocaust.hklaw.com**
The Holocaust Remembrance Essay Contest makes ten one-time awards of $10,000 along with smaller cash prizes.

Monday, May 1

☐ **Jane Austen Society Essay Contest. (9–12) www.jasna.org**
The Jane Austen Society offers a one-time prize of $1,000 for first place in its essay contest.

Monday, May 15

☐ **Society of Women Engineers Scholarship. (12) www.swe.org**
The Society of Women Engineers offers about twenty-five renewable scholarships of up to $5,000 per year to future engineers, male as well as female.

Thursday, June 1

☐ **Arts Recognition and Talent Search, Early Deadline. (11) www.nfaa.org**
The National Foundation for the Advancement of the Arts sponsors the Arts Recognition and Talent Search (ARTS), one of the nation's most prestigious competitions for students in dance, film and video, jazz, music, photography, theater, visual arts, voice, and writing. Hundreds of one-time scholarships up to $25,000 are available. The program is also the gateway to the Presidential Scholars in the Arts recognition program. June 1 is an early deadline with a second round on October 1.

Thursday, June 15

☐ **Hispanic Scholarship Fund/Society of Hispanic Professional Engineers. (12) www.shpe.org/scholarship**
The Hispanic Scholarship Fund and the Society of Hispanic Professional Engineers offer one-time awards of up to $2,500 for students with intended majors in math, computer science, and engineering.

Standardized Testing April–June 2007

Wednesday, April 11

May SAT and Subject Tests, late-registration deadline (approximate)

Friday, April 27

June SAT and Subject Tests, registration deadline (approximate)

Friday, May 4

June ACT, registration deadline

Saturday, May 5

SAT and Subject Tests administered

Wednesday, May 9

June SAT and Subject Tests, late-registration deadline (approximate)

Friday, May 18

June ACT, late-registration deadline

Saturday, June 2

SAT and Subject Tests administered

Saturday, June 9

ACT administered

Coping with the Wait List

The college application process is stressful enough when the answers come back as either a yes or a no. Nothing is more agonizing than getting a maybe—as in, "You've waited four months for our decision and you are really close to getting in, so please stay on our wait list for another month or two."

Colleges use the wait list because they are not sure how many of the accepted applicants will actually enroll. The wait list is their margin of safety to ensure that the class is full. The odds of acceptance from the wait list are generally less than 50/50, but may vary depending on the college and the year. Wait lists are seldom ranked.

Wait-listed students should think hard about whether pursuing admission will be worth the time, effort, and agony. Though most students learn their fate by the end of May, some are left dangling into the summer.

Before doing anything, wait-listed students must send a deposit and communicate their intent to enroll at another institution that did offer an acceptance. There is no need to tell the accepting college about the other college's wait list.

> Set aside time for writing essays and filling out applications. I almost didn't finish my essays before the application deadline because I got bogged down with schoolwork and extracurricular activities.
>
> —Vanderbilt University student

For the wait list, most colleges ask that students return a postcard indicating interest. But that's only the beginning. The wait list is an all-or-nothing proposition that should include one or more of the following, done by mid-April:

- A letter to the admission director communicating an unquenchable desire to attend the college. Strong letters include thoughtful discussion about why the fit is right and updates on any new honors or achievements.

- A campus interview, especially if you have not already had one. Nothing beats a chance to make the case face to face.

- Another recommendation from a current teacher highlighting your achievements in twelfth grade, or a sample of your recent best work.

- A phone call from your college counselor, highlighting the fact that your third-quarter grades are good (they better be) and reinforcing your willingness to attend if accepted.

Unfortunately, many colleges do not have much or any financial aid for wait-listed students. Full-payers are the most likely to get in off the wait list, and those who applied for aid should emphasize their willingness to attend with or without aid if they can realistically do so.

Colleges use spots on the wait list to make dreams come true for a lucky handful who go all-out for admission.

With crying towels at the ready, we offer a few thoughts for Mom and Dad. Most important, be prepared for the continuation of the aloof/emotional/standoffish behavior that may have marked the senior year. Fear of leaving is acted out in strange ways and is not a commentary on your relationship with your son or daughter. Roll with the punches and keep both feet on the ground. As the summer wanes, expect your child to spend every possible moment with friends. They'll miss you too, but don't count on seeing any evidence of that fact. Here are some things to do as the clock winds down:

Loosen the Reigns

We're not suggesting that you compromise major principles or let them run wild. Just ease up a bit. They'll be on their own in a month or two anyway.

Practice your interview with a counselor, teacher, or friend. A firm handshake, clearly articulated speaking, and eye contact goes a long way in making a great first impression.

—Counselor's heads-up

They can spend their last few weeks fighting with you over curfew, or they can begin to adjust to the freedom they will have on campus.

Suggest a Packing List

Mom should fight the temptation to make one. Instead, suggest that your child talk to friends or older peers for ideas about what to bring. Make sure the college has informed you specifically about the dorms and what it thinks your son or daughter will need. Consult with the college before buying a computer.

Discuss Finances

College students are bombarded with credit card applications from the moment they set foot on campus. Now is the time to impart a little financial savvy. What are their prerogatives related to credit cards? Will they open a checking account? How much spending money will they get? All these things should be discussed in advance.

Have Them Attend Orientation

Colleges often have a variety of orientation programs, from a standard campus introduction to weeklong adventure trips. Encourage your son or daughter to do one. A few good friends made at such programs can be a comfort during the initial days of the semester.

> My best interview was less like an interview and more like a conversation.
>
> —Reed College student

Don't Linger When You Drop Them Off

During the first days of college, parents have a status roughly equal to the lepers in Biblical times. We suggest that parents help the student settle in, make sure everything is OK, and then get a move on. When students are insecure about their identity in a new place, the last thing they want is to be seen with Mom and Dad.

Write Letters and Send Email

Every parent wants to keep in touch, but phone calls can be embarrassing when the new student is sitting in a room full of friends. Parents should start out with letters and email and encourage the student to make the first phone call. College students really do want to hear from parents (even if they won't admit it).

Have Realistic Expectations

The first year of college is an emotional roller coaster and far from the carefree time that many of us think we remember. Students should be prepared for some rocky times along with the excitement, and parents should expect at least one or two teary phone calls. Only if the unhappiness persists for a period of months should anyone become concerned.

A final suggestion for parents after they drop off their son or daughter: Do something nice for yourself. Go on a cruise or visit a place you've always wanted to go. Your child will be fine, and you've got a life to live, too.

> Never send in your application without asking someone else to proofread it.
>
> —Counselor's heads-up

A NOTE ON THE APPENDICES

The pages that follow include key deadlines and requirements at the nation's three hundred "best and most interesting" colleges as selected by the *Fiske Guide to Colleges*, where students will find a comprehensive write-up on each.

Appendix A: Standardized Tests
SAT and Subject Tests Calendar—2006–2007
ACT Assessment Calendar 2006–2007
Colleges That Require SAT Subject Tests for Admission
Colleges That Recommend SAT Subject Tests

Appendix B: Admission Deadlines
Early-Decision Deadlines
Early-Action Deadlines
Regular Admission Deadlines

Appendix C: Scholarship Deadlines
Independent Scholarships and Awards
General Interest Scholarships and Awards
Minority Interest Scholarships and Awards
Science and Technology-Related Scholarships and Awards
Essay Contests
Early-Bird Institutional Scholarships

APPENDIX A: STANDARDIZED TESTS

SAT AND SUBJECT TESTS CALENDAR — SPRING 2006

Test Date	Test Offered	Registration Deadline	Late Registration
January 28, 2006	SAT & Subject Tests	December 22, 2005	January 4, 2006
June 3, 2006	SAT only	February 24, 2006	March 8, 2006
May 6, 2006	SAT & Subject Tests	April 3, 2006	April 12, 2006
June 3, 2006	SAT & Subject Tests	April 28, 2006	May 10, 2006

SAT AND SUBJECT TESTS CALENDAR — 2006–2007

Test Date	Test Offered	Approximate Registration Deadline	Approximate Late Registration
October 14, 2006	SAT & Subject Tests	September 13, 2006	September 20, 2006
November 4, 2006	SAT & Subject Tests	September 29, 2006	October 11, 2006
December 2, 2006	SAT & Subject Tests	October 27, 2006	November 8, 2006
January 27, 2007	SAT & Subject Tests	December 21, 2006	January 3, 2007
March 10, 2007	SAT only	February 2, 2007	February 14, 2007
May 5, 2007	SAT & Subject Tests	April 2, 2007	April 11, 2007
June 2, 2007	SAT & Subject Tests	April 27, 2007	May 9, 2007

At press time, the College Board had not released the registration and late-registration deadlines for 2006–2007. The dates above are projections based on past years. Visit www.collegeboard.com to confirm these dates.

All dates are postmark deadlines for students in the United States. (Receipt dates for those outside the U.S.) Students can also register at www.collegeboard.com. For students who cannot test on Saturday for religious reasons, the tests will be offered on the Sunday immediately following. March and April test dates are available only in the U.S.

ACT ASSESSMENT CALENDAR—SPRING 2006

Test Date	Registration Deadline	Late Registration
February 11, 2006**	January 6, 2006	January 20, 2006
April 8, 2006	March 3, 2006	March 17, 2006
June 10, 2006	May 5, 2006	May 19, 2006

** Not available in the state of New York.
All dates are postmark deadlines.

ACT ASSESSMENT CALENDAR—2006–2007

Test Date	Registration Deadline	Late Registration
September 16, 2006*	August 18, 2006	August 25, 2006
October 28, 2006	September 22, 2006	September 23, 2006
December 9, 2006	November 3, 2006	November 16, 2006
February 10, 2007**	January 5, 2007	January 19, 2007
April 14, 2007	March 9, 2007	March 23, 2007
June 9, 2007	May 4, 2007	May 18, 2007

*Available only in Arizona, California, Florida, Georgia, Illinois, Indiana, Maryland, Nevada, North Carolina, Pennsylvania, South Carolina, Texas, and Washington.

**Not available in the state of New York.
All dates are postmark deadlines. www.act.org

COLLEGES THAT REQUIRE SAT SUBJECT TESTS FOR ADMISSION

Institutions requiring Subject Tests are confined to the East Coast and California. The colleges below require either two or three tests, as noted below. Some colleges allow students to choose any test; others stipulate particular ones. Many colleges allow students to submit an ACT score instead of one or more Subject Test scores.

Amherst College (2)
Barnard College (2)
Boston College (2)
Boston University (2)
Brandeis University (2)
Brown University (2)
Bryn Mawr College (2)
University of California (all campuses) (2)
California Institute of Technology (2)
Carnegie Mellon University (2)
Catholic University (placement only)
Columbia University (2)
Connecticut College (2)
Cooper Union (engineering only) (2)
Cornell University (2)
Dartmouth College (2)
Duke University (2)
Georgetown University (3)

Harvard University (3)
Harvey Mudd College (2)
Haverford College (2)
Massachusetts Institute of Technology (3)
Northwestern University Integrated Science Program (3)
   and Honors Program in Medical Education (2)
University of Pennsylvania (2)
Pomona College (2)
Princeton University (3)
Rice University (2)
Swarthmore College (2)
Vassar College (2)
University of Virginia (2)
Washington & Lee University (2)
Wellesley College (2)
Wesleyan University (2)
Williams College (2)
Yale University (3)

COLLEGES THAT RECOMMEND SAT SUBJECT TESTS

Students who are required to take Subject Tests by other institutions should forward their scores to these colleges. Students not otherwise planning to take Subject Tests should consult with these colleges as to whether they should take the tests. Some colleges ask for Subject scores only for placement. Students who are taking the ACT may be able to submit scores from it in lieu of taking the Subject Tests.

American University
Babson College
Carleton College
Case Western Reserve University
Davidson College
Eckerd College
University of Georgia
Hamilton College
Hood College
Johns Hopkins University
Marlboro College
Mary Washington College
Mills College
New York University
University of North Carolina at Chapel Hill
Northwestern University
Oberlin College

Occidental College
Ohio Wesleyan University
Pitzer College
Reed College
University of Rochester
Rollins College
Skidmore College
Smith College
University of Southern California
Southern Methodist University (some programs)
Stanford University
Stevens Institute of Technology
Sweet Briar College
University of Texas at Austin
Wheaton College (IL)
Whitman College
College of William & Mary

APPENDIX B: ADMISSION DEADLINES

ED applicants are obligated to attend the college if accepted. Students may apply to only one college via early decision and must withdraw all other applications if accepted. Some colleges have two early-decision deadlines. In such cases, the second ED deadline is denoted with a (II).

October 1
University of Florida

October 15
George Washington University (part I)

November 1
Boston University
Brown University
Carnegie Mellon University (fine arts only)
Columbia University
Cornell University
Dartmouth College
Denison University
DePauw University
Duke University
Elon University
Emory University
Ithaca College
Miami University (OH)
University of Miami (FL)
New York University
Northwestern University
University of Pennsylvania

Princeton University
Rhodes College
Rice University
University of Rochester
St. Olaf College
Scripps College
Southwestern University
State University of New York at Buffalo
Stetson University
Trinity University (TX)
Tulane University
Vanderbilt University
University of Virginia
Virginia Tech
Wellesley College
College of William and Mary

November 10
Williams College

November 15
Agnes Scott College
Albion College
Allegheny College

American University
Amherst College
Antioch College
Babson College
Barnard College
Bates College
Bennington College
Bowdoin College
Brandeis University
Bryn Mawr College
Bucknell University
Carleton College
Carnegie Mellon University
Claremont McKenna College
Clark University
Colby College
Colgate University
Colorado College
Connecticut College ·
Davidson College
University of Delaware
Dickinson College
Eugene Lang College
Fairfield University
Fordham University
Franklin & Marshall College
Furman University
George Washington University (part II)
Gettysburg College
Goucher College
Guilford College
Gustavus Adolphus College
Hamilton College
Hampden-Sydney College
Hampshire College

Hartwick College
Harvey Mudd College
Haverford College
Hobart and William Smith Colleges
Hood College
Johns Hopkins University
Kalamazoo College
Lawrence University
Lehigh University
Macalester College
Marlboro College
Middlebury College
Morehouse College
Mount Holyoke College
College of New Jersey
Oberlin College
Occidental College
Pomona College
University of Puget Sound
Randolph-Macon Woman's College
Reed College
Rensselaer Polytechnic Institute
University of Richmond
Rollins College
St. Lawrence University
Sarah Lawrence College
Smith College
University of the South (Sewanee)
State University of New York–Geneseo
Stevens Institute of Technology
Swarthmore College
Syracuse University
Trinity College (CT)
Tufts University
Union College

Vassar College
Wabash College
Wake Forest University
Warren Wilson College
Washington University in St. Louis
Washington & Lee University
Wesleyan University
Wheaton College (MA)
Whitman College
Wittenberg University
Wofford College
Worcester Polytechnic Institute

November 20
Grinnell College

December 1
Alfred University
College of the Atlantic
Austin College
Clarkson University
Cooper Union (art and engineering only)
Drew University
Earlham College
Gordon College
Hiram College
Hollins University
Kenyon College
Lake Forest College
Manhattanville College
Ohio Wesleyan University

Rochester Institute of Technology
St. Mary's College of Maryland
Skidmore College
Sweet Briar College
Washington & Jefferson College
College of Wooster

December 5
Presbyterian College

December 15
College of the Holy Cross
University of Puget Sound (II)
Middlebury College (II)
Susquehanna University
Wells College

December 29
Pomona College (II)

January 1
Bates College (II)
Bennington College (II)
Bowdoin College (II)
Bryn Mawr College (II)
Bucknell University (II)
Claremont McKenna College (II)
Colby College (II)
Colorado College (II)
Connecticut College (II)
Davidson College (II)

Denison University (II)
Emory University (II)
Grinnell College (II)
Hamilton College (II)
Hobart and William Smith Colleges (II)
Lafayette College
Lehigh University (II)
Macalester College (II)
Mount Holyoke College (II)
Oberlin College (II)
Reed College (II)
Rhodes College (II)
Sarah Lawrence College (II)
Scripps College (II)
Smith College (II)
Southwestern University (II)
Swarthmore College (II)
Tufts University (II)
Vanderbilt University (II)
Vassar College (II)
Washington & Lee University (II)
Washington University in St. Louis (II)
Wesleyan University (II)
Whitman College (II)
Worcester Polytechnic Institute (II)

January 10
College of the Atlantic (II)

January 15
Carleton College (II)
Clarkson University (II)
Colgate University (II)
Dickinson College (II)
Drew University (II)
Franklin & Marshall College (II)
Gettysburg College (II)
Hartwick College (II)
Kalamazoo College (II)
Kenyon College (II)
University of Richmond (II)
Rollins College (II)
St. Lawrence University (II)
Skidmore College (II)
Stevens Institute of Technology (II)
Trinity College (CT) (II)
Union College (II)
Ursinus College
Wheaton College (MA) (II)
College of Wooster (II)

February 1
Muhlenberg College

EARLY-ACTION DEADLINES

Applying EA does not obligate students to attend if accepted. Students may weigh other offers until the May 1 reply date. Some colleges have two early-action deadlines. In such cases, the second EA deadline is denoted with a (II).

A few universities with EA programs, notably Harvard, Yale, and Stanford, forbid students who apply EA from applying early to another institution. This program, known as "single choice early action," is relatively new. Check with the college if you are in doubt as to whether you retain the right to apply early at another institution.

October 15
Harvard University (recommended)
University of Georgia

November 1
Alma College
Auburn University
Bard College
Boston College
California Institute of Technology
Case Western Reserve University
University of Denver
Fordham University
Georgetown University
Howard University
James Madison University
University of Massachusetts at Amherst
Massachusetts Institute of Technology
University of Miami (FL)
University of North Carolina at Chapel Hill
North Carolina State University
University of Notre Dame
Santa Clara University
Southern Methodist University
Stanford University
University of Tennessee
Trinity University (TX)

Tulane University
University of Vermont
Villanova University
Wheaton College (IL)
Willamette University
Yale University

November 10
Elon University

November 15
Albertson College
University of Arkansas
Babson College
Beloit College
Catholic University
University of Chicago
Colorado College
DePaul University
Lewis and Clark College
Mills College
University of Minnesota at Morris
University of the Pacific
Pepperdine University
Pitzer College
University of San Francisco
Spelman College

State University of New York at Binghamton
Texas Christian University
Truman State University
Worcester Polytechnic Institute

November 28
University of North Carolina at Asheville

December 1
Albion College
Antioch College
Austin College
Birmingham Southern College
Butler University
Centre College
University of Connecticut
Cornell College
University of Dallas
Depauw University
Dickinson College
Goucher College
Hampshire College
Hood College
Kalamazoo College
Knox College
Lake Forest College
Lawrence University
University of Maryland
Millsaps College
University of New Hampshire
Rice University
St. John's University (MN)
St. Olaf College
Simmons College
Whittier College

Willamette University (II)
Wittenberg University

December 5
Oglethorpe University

December 15
Beloit College (II)
Ohio Wesleyan University
University of Redlands
University of Rhode Island
Rhode Island School of Design
Trinity University (TX) (II)
Wabash College
Wells College

January 1
Earlham College
Grinnell College
Hartwick College
Hobart and William Smith Colleges (II)
Wellesley College
Worcester Polytechnic Institute (II)

January 15
Austin College (II)
Guilford College
Gustavus Adolphus College
Hampden-Sydney College
Illinois Institute of Technology
Marlboro College
Mary Washington College
Washington and Jefferson College
Xavier University (LA)

November 15
Deep Springs College
University of Illinois at Urbana-Champaign

November 30
University of California (all campuses)
Pennsylvania State University (priority)

December 1
George Washington University (part 1)
Marquette University (priority)
University of Maryland (priority)
Rutgers—The State University of New Jersey (priority)
University of South Carolina (priority)
University of Washington

December 15
Connecticut College (part I)
Middlebury College (part I)
University of Minnesota (priority)
Stanford University

January 1
Amherst College
Barnard College
Bennington College
Boston College
Boston University
Bowdoin College
Brown University
Bucknell University

California Institute of Technology
Carnegie Mellon University
University of Chicago
Claremont McKenna College
Colby College
Columbia University
Connecticut College (part II)
Cooper Union (architecture only)
Cornell University
Dartmouth College
Davidson College
University of Dayton (priority)
Duke University
Hamilton College
Harvard University
James Madison University
Johns Hopkins University
Lafayette College
Lehigh University
Massachusetts Institute of Technology
Middlebury College (part II)
University of Notre Dame
Northwestern University
University of Pennsylvania
Pomona College
Princeton University
Rensselaer Polytechnic Institute
Sarah Lawrence College
Swarthmore College
Syracuse University
Tufts University
Vanderbilt University

Vassar College
University of Virginia
Wesleyan University
College of William & Mary
Williams College
Yale University

January 7
Villanova University

January 10
Cooper Union (art only)
Elon University
Georgetown University
Occidental College
Rice University
University of Southern California

January 15
Babson College
Bard College
Bates College
Beloit College
Birmingham-Southern College
Brandeis University
Bryn Mawr College
Carleton College
Case Western Reserve University
University of Cincinnati
Colgate University
Colorado College
University of Colorado at Boulder
University of Dallas
University of Delaware

University of Denver
Lehigh University
Emerson College
Emory University
Fairfield University
University of Florida
Furman University
George Washington University (part II)
Georgia Institute of Technology
Hampshire College
Harvey Mudd College
Haverford College
College of the Holy Cross
Kalamazoo College (II)
Kenyon College
Lawrence University
Macalester College
University of Massachusetts at Amherst
McGill University
Mount Holyoke College
State University of New York at Geneseo
New York University
Northeastern University
University of North Carolina at Chapel Hill
Oberlin College
University of the Pacific
Pepperdine University
Pitzer College
Reed College
University of Richmond
University of Rochester
St. Mary's College of Maryland
Santa Clara University
Scripps College
Skidmore College

Smith College
Southern Methodist University
State University of New York at Binghamton
University of Tennessee
Trinity College (CT)
Tulane University
Union College
University of Vermont
Virginia Tech
Wake Forest University
Washington & Lee University
Washington University in St. Louis
Wellesley College
Wheaton College (IL)
Wheaton College (MA)
Whitman College

January 20
Grinnell College
University of Maryland
University of Rochester

January 31
Miami University (OH)

February 1
Alfred University
American University
Antioch College
Centre College
Clark University

Cooper Union (engineering only)
Denison University
DePaul University
DePauw University
Dickinson College
Eugene Lang College
Fordham University
Franklin & Marshall College
George Mason University
Goucher College
Hiram College
Hobart and William Smith Colleges
Hood College
Indiana University
Knox College
Lewis and Clark College
Marquette University
Mary Washington College
University of Miami (FL)
University of Michigan
Mills College
Millsaps College
New College of Florida (priority)
University of New Hampshire
North Carolina State University
Ohio University
Prescott College
Rhodes College
Rochester Institute of Technology
St. Olaf College
University of San Francisco
University of the South (Sewanee)

Spelman College
State University of New York–Geneseo
Sweet Briar College
Texas A&M University
University of Texas at Austin
Trinity University (TX)
Wabash College
Whittier College
Willamette University
University of Wisconsin at Madison
Wofford College
Worcester Polytechnic Institute

February 15

Allegheny College
University of Arkansas
College of the Atlantic
Brigham Young University
Catholic University
Drew University
Earlham College
Gettysburg College
Guilford College
Hartwick College
Hollins University (priority)
Howard University
Illinois Wesleyan University
Kalamazoo College
University of Kentucky
Morehouse College
Muhlenberg College
College of New Jersey
University of the Pacific
Rhode Island School of Design

Rollins College
St. John's University (MN)
St. Lawrence University
University of South Carolina
Southwestern University
State University of New York at Stony Brook
Stevens Institute of Technology
Texas Christian University
Ursinus College
College of Wooster

February 28

Queens College (CAN)

March 1

Agnes Scott College
Austin College
University of Connecticut
Evergreen State College
Florida State University
Gordon College
Hampden-Sydney College
Ithaca College
Lake Forest College
Manhattanville College
Marlboro College
University of North Carolina at Asheville
University of North Carolina at Greensboro
Ohio Wesleyan University
University of Oregon
Oregon State University
Purdue University
Randolph-Macon Woman's College
University of Rhode Island

Rose-Hulman Institute of Technology
St. John's College (MD & NM)
Susquehanna University
University of Toronto
Truman State University
Washington & Jefferson College
Wells College
West Virginia University

March 15

Clarkson University
University of Minnesota at Morris
Ripon College
Stetson University
Warren Wilson College
Wittenberg University

March 31

University of British Columbia

April 1

University of Arizona
Eckerd College
University of Iowa
Gustavus Adolphus College
Howard University

May 1

College of Charleston
Clemson University
University of Hawaii at Manoa
State University of New York at Albany
Texas Tech University
University of Utah

June 1

Albertson College
Albion College
Colorado School of Mines
University of Oklahoma

APPENDIX C: SCHOLARSHIP DEADLINES

INDEPENDENT SCHOLARSHIPS AND AWARDS

These awards come from non-college sources and can therefore be used to cover costs at any institution in the country. All such awards mentioned in this book are listed here. We divide them into five categories: General Interest, Minority Interest, Science and Technology-Related Scholarships, and Prizes, Essay Contests, and Early-Bird Institutional Scholarships. Each list is in chronological order by deadline. Dates are for 2006 and may vary in succeeding years. Since deadlines are subject to change, we strongly recommend that you consult the websites referenced below for the latest information. For an overview of each award, consult the description of the appropriate week in the calendar.

This book lists many of the nation's most prestigious scholarships and prizes, but it does not provide a comprehensive list of all independent scholarships. For further information on the scholarship search, see the *Fiske Guide to Getting into the Right College*.

GENERAL INTEREST SCHOLARSHIPS AND AWARDS

January 7
Discover Card Tribute Award.
  www.discovercard.com/tribute.htm

January 13
Elks Most Valuable Student Scholarship.
  www.elks.org/enf/scholars/mvs.cfm

January 15
Phi Delta Kappa International Scholarship.
  www.pdkintl.org/studser/sschol.htm

January 20
National Honor Society Scholarship. www.nhs.us

January 31
Papa John's Scholars. www.papajohnsscholars.com
Navy ROTC Scholarship. www.todaysmilitary.com

February 1
Jaycee War Memorial Fund Scholarship.
  www.usjaycees.org/scholarships.htm
Sam Walton Community Scholarship.
  www.walmartfoundation.org
Junior Achievement Scholarship. www.ja.org
DAR Scholarships. www.dar.org

February 5
American Foreign Service Association Scholarship.
  www.afsa.org

General Interest Scholarships and Awards, continued

February 17
National Alliance for Scholastic Achievement Scholarship.
www.eee.org/bus/nasa

February 20
USA Today All-USA Academic Team.
www.usatoday.com

March 1
Donna Reed Performing Arts Scholarships.
www.donnareed.org
Pfizer Epilepsy Scholarship. www.epilepsy-scholarship.com
Sons of the American Revolution Rumbaugh Oration
Contest. www.sar.org

March 5
Scholar Athlete Milk Mustache of the Year (SAMMY)
Award. www.whymilk.com

March 15
U.S.A. Funds Access to Education Scholarship.
www.usafunds.org
Horace Mann Student Scholarship Program.
www.horacemann.com
NFIB Free Enterprise Scholarship
www.nfib.com

March 22
Young American Creative Patriotic Art Award.
www.ladiesauxvfw.com

April 1
Yoshiyama Award. www.hitachi.org/yoshiyama

April 15
AMVETS National Scholarship. www.amvets.org

April 30
The Tylenol Scholarship. scholarship.tylenol.com

June 1
NFAA Arts Recognition and Talent Search (ARTS), Early
Deadline. www.artsawards.org

October 1
NFAA Arts Recognition and Talent Search (ARTS), Final
Deadline. www.artsawards.org

October 15
Outstanding Students of America Scholarship.
www.outstandingstudentsofamerica.com
Horatio Alger Scholarship Program. www.horatioalger.com

October 31

Coca-Cola Scholars Deadline. www.coca-colascholars.org

Prudential Spirit of Community Awards Deadline.
www.principals.org

November 1

VFW Voice of Democracy Scholarship.
www.vfw.org/yourtown/you_VoiceOf.htm

Target All-Around Scholarship. www.target.com

November 11

Susan G. Komen Breast Cancer Foundation College
Scholarship. www.komen.org/grants

November 15

Army ROTC Scholarship. www.armyrotc.com

November 30

National Security Agency, Undergraduate Training Program.
www.nsa.gov

Defense Intelligence Agency Undergraduate Training
Assistance Program. www.dia.mil

December 1

Toyota Community Scholars. www.toyota.com

Air Force ROTC Scholarship. www.afrotc.com

December 5

NASSP Principal's Leadership Award. www.principals.org

December 11

National Academy of Television Arts and Sciences
Scholarship. www.emmyonline.org/emmy/scholr.html

December 10

National Beta Club Scholarship. www.betaclub.org

December 15

AXA Achievement Scholarship.
www.axa-achievement.com

Burger King Scholars Program. www.burgerking.com

Deadline Varies

Scholastic Art and Writing Awards.
www.scholastic.com/artandwritingawards

National History Day. www.nationalhistoryday.org

Junior Science and Humanities Symposium. www.jshs.org

U.S. Senate Youth Scholarship. (11–12).
www.isbe.net/hearst

Minority Interest Scholarships and Awards

January 9
Ron Brown Scholar Program. African Americans.
www.ronbrown.org

January 13
Gates Millennium Scholarship. www.gmsp.org

April 1
Jackie Robinson Foundation Scholarship.
www.jackierobinson.org

June 15
Hispanic Scholarship Fund/Society of Hispanic Professional
Engineers Scholarship Program. www.shpe.org/scholarship

October 1
Hispanic Scholarship Fund/Toyota Scholarship Program.
www.hsf.net/scholarship/seniors.php

December 15
Hispanic Scholarship Fund High School Scholarship.
www.hsf.net/scholarships.php

Science and Technology-Related Scholarships and Awards

January 15
USDA 1890 National Scholars Program.
1890scholars.program.usda.gov
Young Naturalist Awards.
www.amnh.org/nationalcenter/youngnaturalistawards

February 1
Toshiba/NSTA ExploraVision Awards.
www.exploravision.org

May 15
Society of Women Engineers Scholarship. www.swe.org

June 15
Hispanic Scholarship Fund/Society of Hispanic Professional
Engineers Scholarship Program. www.shpe.org/scholarship

October 1
Hispanic Scholarship Fund/Toyota Scholarship Program.
www.hsf.net/scholarship/seniors.php

October 2
Siemens Westinghouse Competition in Math, Science, and
Technology. www.siemens-foundation.org

November 16
Intel Science Talent Search. www.sciserv.org/isef

December 1
SAE Engineering Scholarship. www.sae.org

Deadline Varies
Intel Science and Engineering Fairs. www.sciserv.org/isef

Essay Contests

January 7
JFK Profile in Courage Essay Contest. www.jfkcontest.org

January 13
United Nations Association National High School Essay
Contest. www.unausa.org

January 17
The DuPont Challenge Science Essay Contest.
www.glcomm.com/dupont

February 1
U.S. Institute of Peace National Peace Essay Contest.
www.usip.org/ed/npec/index.html

February 15
EF Global Citizen Essay Contest. School nomination
required. www.eftours.com

February 28
Optimist International Essay Contest. www.optimist.org

March 1
Kaplan/Newsweek "My Turn" Essay Contest.
www.kaptest.com/essay
American Foreign Service Essay Contest. www.afsa.org

April 25
Ayn Rand Essay Contest. www.aynrand.org/contests

April 30
Holocaust Remembrance Project Essay Contest.
www.holocaust.hklaw.com

May 1
Jane Austen Society Essay Contest. www.jasna.org

June 6
Chemagination Essay Contest. www.chemistry.org

November 23
Guideposts Young Writers Contest.
www.guideposts.com/young_writers_contest.asp

December 5
American Fire Sprinkler Association Essay Contest.
www.afsascholarship.org

December 31
Sons of American Revolution Knight Essay Contest.
www.sar.org
Mensa MERF Essay Contest.
www.merf.us.mensa.org/scholarships/index.php

EARLY BIRD INSTITUTIONAL SCHOLARSHIPS

Institutional scholarships are sponsored by a college or university rather than an independent group. Since you can't take them anywhere aside from the institution that offers them, such scholarships tend to be easier to win than independent ones. And they also tend to be more lucrative. Unless otherwise noted, the scholarships in this list are renewable for four years, unlike most independent scholarships, which are one-time deals.

Many institutional scholarships are available to any applicant who applies for admission. But some awards require an early application. The following list includes institutional scholarships with a deadline before January 1—the kind that so often sneak up on unsuspecting applicants. Since deadlines are subject to change, we strongly recommend that you consult the colleges below for the latest information.

Some of the entries below are for a particular scholarship program. Others are general scholarship deadlines, meaning that some or all of the institution's scholarships are available only—or on a priority basis—to students who apply by the deadline noted. When grades and test scores are cited, such figures are the minimums for consideration.

Spring of Eleventh Grade

University of Dallas. Aspiring Scholars Award Program. Criteria: 11th graders must attend an on-campus program in February, April, or June. Amount: up to $8,000. www.udallas.edu

September 20

Davidson College. Bryan Scholars. Criteria: excellence in athletics and academics. Amount: $25,000. www.davidson.edu

October 1

University of North Carolina at Chapel Hill. Morehead Scholarship Nomination Deadline (participating schools only). Criteria: all-around excellence. Amount: full costs of attendance and summer stipend. www.moreheadfoundation.org

October 15

Whittier College. Honors Weekend application deadline. Criteria: 3.5 GPA and 1200 SAT or 27 ACT. Amount: up to full tuition. www.whittier.edu

Washington University in St. Louis. Danforth Scholars. Criteria: all-around excellence. Amount: up to full tuition. School nomination required. www.wustl.edu

Boston University. Scholarship Examination Competition registration deadline (approximate). High scorers on early-November multiple-choice exam are eligible for scholarships up to full tuition. Multiple-choice exam for full-tuition scholars to BU's college of engineering. www.bu.edu

October 31

Georgia Institute of Technology—Presidential Scholarship. Criteria: academic excellence and leadership. Amount: up to the full costs of attendance. www.gatech.edu

November 1

Boston College. Presidential Scholars. Criteria: academic excellence, leadership, community service. Amount: scholarships up to full tuition. www.bc.edu

Emory University. Emory Scholars. Criteria: all-around excellence. Amount: up to full costs of attendance. School nomination required. www.emory.edu

Howard University. General scholarship deadline. Criteria: varies. Amount: up to the full costs of attendance. www.howard.edu

Indiana University. General scholarship priority deadline. Criteria: varies. Amount: up to full costs. www.indiana.edu

Kansas State University. General scholarship deadline. Criteria and amounts vary. www.ksu.edu

Miami University (OH). Harrison Scholars. Criteria: all-around excellence. Amount: up to the full costs of attendance. www.muohio.edu

University of Michigan. General scholarship priority deadline. Criteria: varies. Amount: up to $10,000. www.umich.edu

Michigan State University. Alumni Distinguished Scholarships. Criteria: academic excellence. Amount: up to the full costs of attendance. www.msu.edu

North Carolina State University. Park Scholarship. Criteria: all-around excellence. Amount: up to the full costs of attendance. School nomination required where applicable. www.ncsu.edu

University of North Carolina at Chapel Hill. Pogue Scholarships. Criteria: All-around excellence, special emphasis on minority applicants. Amount: $7,500. www.unc.edu

University of Oklahoma. General scholarship deadline. Some scholarships awarded as early as November. Criteria and amounts vary. www.ou.edu

Rhodes College. Bellingrath Scholarship Nomination. Criteria: all-around excellence. Amount: up to the full costs of attendance. Nomination required. www.rhodes.edu

Scripps College. James E. Scripps Scholarships. Criteria: all-around excellence. Amount: half of tuition. www.scripps-college.edu

University of Tennessee. General scholarship deadline. Criteria and amounts vary. www.utk.edu

Villanova University. Presidential Scholarship. Criteria: 3.8 GPA and 1400 SAT or 32 ACT. Amount: full tuition. www.villanova.edu

University of Virginia. Jefferson Scholars Nomination. Criteria: all-around excellence. Amount: up to full costs of attendance and summer stipend. School nomination required where applicable. www.jeffersonscholars.org

November 15

DePaul University. General scholarship deadline. Criteria: varies. Amount: up to $13,000. www.depaul.edu

University of Georgia. Foundation Fellows. Criteria: 1400 SAT or 31 ACT. Amount: up to $14,000. www.uga.edu

Louisiana State University. General scholarship deadline. Criteria: varies. Amount: up to $3,000. www.lsu.edu

University of San Francisco. University Scholars. Criteria: 3.8 GPA and 1320 SAT or 30 ACT. Amount: $16,000. www.usfca.edu

November 28

University of North Carolina at Asheville. University Laurels Scholarships. Criteria: 3.5 GPA and 1250 SAT or 28 ACT. Amount: up to the full costs of attendance. www.unca.edu

December 1

University of Alabama. General scholarship deadline. Criteria: academic excellence. Amount: varies. www.ua.edu

Auburn University. General scholarship deadline. Criteria: academic excellence. Amount: up to $10,500. www.auburn.edu.

Boston University. Trustee Scholarship. Criteria: all-around excellence. Amount: full tuition. School nomination required. www.bu.edu

Butler University. Departmental Scholarships. Criteria: varies. Amount: $2,000–$3,000. www.butler.edu

University of Connecticut. General scholarship deadline. Criteria: varies. Amount: up to $9,800. www.uconn.edu

Fairfield University. General scholarship deadline. Criteria: varies. Amount: up to $16,000. www.fairfield.edu

University of Iowa. Presidential and Dean's Scholarships. Criteria: academic excellence. Amount: $7,000 and $1,000, respectively. www.uiowa.edu

Loyola University New Orleans. General scholarship deadline. Criteria: academic excellence, artistic talent. Amount: up to $14,000. www.loyno.edu

University of Maryland at College Park. General scholarship deadline. Criteria and amounts vary. www.umd.edu

Millsaps College. Presidential and Second Century Scholarships. Criteria: all-around excellence. Amount: up to $25,000. www.millsaps.edu

University of Missouri at Columbia. General scholarship deadline. Criteria: varies. Amount: $7,500. www.missouri.edu

University of Missouri at Rolla. General scholarship deadline. Criteria: academic excellence. Amount: varies. www.umr.edu

University of New Mexico. Regents and Presidential Scholarships. Criteria: academic excellence. Amount: Up to the full costs of attendance. www.unm.edu

Purdue University. Beering School of Science Scholarships. Criteria and amounts vary. www.purdue.edu

Randolph-Macon Woman's College. Presidential Scholarships. Criteria: all-around excellence. Amount: up to the full costs of attendance with travel stipend. www.rmwc.edu

Rutgers–The State University of New Jersey. General scholarship deadline. Criteria: varies. Amount: up to $15,000. www.rutgers.edu

University of South Carolina. General scholarship deadline. Criteria: academic excellence. Amount: up to $12,000. www.sc.edu

St. Louis University. General scholarship deadline. Criteria: varies. Amount: up to full tuition. www.slu.edu

University of Texas at Austin. General scholarship deadline. Criteria and amounts vary. www.utexas.edu

Wake Forest University. Reynolds Scholarships. Criteria: all-around excellence. Amount: full costs of attendance and summer stipend. www.wfu.edu

December 5

Oglethorpe College. JEO Scholarship. Criteria: 3.75 GPA and 1360 SAT or 31 ACT. Amount: full costs of attendance. www.oglethorpe.edu

Presbyterian College. General scholarship deadline. Criteria: varies. Amount: up to full costs of attendance. www.presbyterian.edu

December 10

University of Southern California. General scholarship deadline. Criteria: varies. Amount: up to full tuition. www.usc.edu

December 15

Ithaca College. Park Scholarship in journalism and communications. Criteria: top 5 percent and 1300 SAT. Amount: up to the full costs of attendance. www.ithaca.edu

Kenyon College. Honor and Science Scholarships. Criteria: varies. Amount: up to half tuition. www.kenyon.edu

Ohio State University. University Scholar Maximus Scholarships. Criteria: varies. Amount: up to the full costs of attendance. www.osu.edu

University of Redlands. General scholarship deadline. Criteria: varies. Amount: from $500 to $10,000. www.redlands.edu

University of Rhode Island. Centennial Scholarships. Criteria: Class rank in top third and 1150 SAT or 25 ACT. Amount: up to full tuition. www.uri.edu

University of Richmond. Oldham Scholarship and Ethyl and Albemarle Science Scholarship. Criteria: all-around excellence. Amount: Full costs of attendance and summer stipend. www.richmond.edu

Tulane University. Dean's Honor Scholarship. Criteria: 1450 SAT I or 33 ACT. Amount: full tuition. www.tulane.edu

Wabash College. President's Scholarships. Criteria: class rank top 20 percent and 1150 SAT or 25 ACT. Amount: $2,500-$12,500. www.wabash.edu

Washington & Lee University. George Washington Honor Scholarship. Criteria: all-around excellence. Amount: up to the full costs of attendance. www.wlu.edu

December 31

Clemson University. General scholarship deadline. Criteria and amounts vary. www.clemson.edu

GLOSSARY

The language of college admission is replete with arcane acronyms and obscure terms. Here are some definitions.

ACT: A nonprofit organization that administers the standardized test that bears its name. Most colleges allow students to submit results from either the ACT or the SAT to satisfy the standardized testing requirement. ACT is not affiliated with the College Board or ETS.

Advanced Placement (AP): Courses taught under the aegis of the College Board Advanced Placement Program. These courses follow a standard curriculum and culminate in exams scored on a scale of 1–5. High scores qualify students for credit at participating colleges.

College Board: Also known as the College Entrance Examination Board, the College Board produces the Preliminary SAT (PSAT), the SAT, and the Subject Tests. The College Board also runs the Advanced Placement (AP) Program and one of its subdivisions, the College Scholarship Service, is the maker of the CSS/Financial Aid PROFILE. See also: Educational Testing Service.

Common Application: A standard application form that is accepted by more than two hundred selective colleges in lieu of their own form. Available at www.commonapp.org and in high school guidance offices.

consortium: A group of colleges or universities that offer joint programs or allow students from one institution to take courses at another.

CSS/Financial Aid PROFILE: A financial aid form produced by the College Board that is required for students seeking aid at approximately 10 percent of the nation's four-year colleges (including most highly selective institutions).

deferral: The term applied to applications for early action or early decision that are deferred for consideration with the regular application pool.

demonstrated need: The difference between the Expected Family Contribution (EFC) and the total cost of attendance at a particular institution.

early action: A program whereby students receive an early-admission decision, but are not obligated to enroll if admitted. Also known as early notification.

early decision: A program that gives students an early admission decision with the obligation to enroll if admitted and to withdraw applications from other institutions.

Educational Testing Service (ETS): A nonprofit organization that designs and administers the SAT I and II through a contractual arrangement with the College Board.

federal methodology (FM): The method of calculating the Expected Family Contribution (EFC) that rests solely on the data submitted in the Free Application for Federal Student Aid (FAFSA) and the federal aid formula.

financial aid package: The bundle of aid awarded by a particular college that may include grants, loans, and a work-study job.

Free Application for Federal Student Aid (FAFSA): A financial aid form produced by the federal government that is required for students seeking aid by nearly all colleges and universities.

institutional methodology (IM): A method of calculating Expected Family Contribution (EFC) that varies by college and may depend on data submitted in the Free Application for Federal Student Aid (FAFSA), the CSS/Financial Aid PROFILE, and the college's own aid form.

institutional scholarship: A scholarship awarded by a college or university. Generally available only to students who plan to enroll.

International Baccalaureate (IB): A program offered by schools in more than one hundred nations that covers six academic areas in the final two years of high school, culminating in an IB diploma. In the U.S., participation in IB is relatively small compared to AP.

National Merit Scholarship Program: A scholarship and recognition program based primarily on scores from the Preliminary SAT (PSAT). More than 7,500 students each year receive scholarships based on National Merit status, ranging from several hundred dollars to the full costs of attendance. Separate programs honor African-American and Hispanic students.

need-blind admission: The term that applies to colleges that make admission decisions without regard to the financial circumstances of the applicants. Colleges with need-blind admission do not necessarily offer aid to meet the full need of all accepted applicants.

PLAN: A test produced by ACT that is administered by schools in the fall of 10th grade. PLAN can help predict ACT scores.

preferential packaging: A method of awarding financial aid in which colleges offer the best aid packages to their most desired applicants.

Preliminary SAT (PSAT): A test produced by the College Board that is administered by high schools to eleventh graders and some tenth graders. The PSAT is the qualifying test for consideration in the National Merit Scholarship Program.

Reserve Officer Training Corps (ROTC): A program that offers scholarships up to full tuition at hundreds of colleges nationwide. Students earn a degree while training part-time for military service. After graduation, students are generally required to serve on active duty for four years. Offered by the Army, Navy, and Air Force.

rolling admission: The term describing admission without fixed application deadlines. Applications are evaluated as they are received until the class is full.

SAT and Subject Tests: Formerly known as SAT I, the SAT is a three-hour test that consists of verbal and math sections. The Subject Tests, formerly known as SAT IIs and Achievement Tests, are one-hour tests devoted to particular subjects.

self-help: A term that describes the portion of a financial aid package consisting of loans and wages from a work-study job.

Student Aid Report (SAR): A form send to families in response to submission of the Free Application for Federal Student Aid (FAFSA) that includes the Expected Family Contribution (EFC), a figure that may be modified at colleges that use institutional methodology (IM).

wait list (or waitlist): A list of applicants to a particular college who are not admitted in the regular-decision pool, but who may be considered if space is still available after admitted students have indicated whether or not they will attend.

work study: A federally funded program wherein students are given campus jobs with the wages calculated as part of their financial aid package.

yield: The percentage of accepted applicants at a particular college who choose to enroll.

ACKNOWLEDGMENTS

We are grateful to many people who assisted in the publication of this book. The members of the Fiske College Counselors Advisory Group, listed below, provided important input. They were our source for the "Counselor's heads-up" advice, and students and parents from their school communities are also quoted in the text.

We are grateful to Laura Johnson Frey for her thorough reading of the first edition of the book. Mary Anne Modzelewski, Bruce's colleague at Sandia Preparatory School, has been an important source of support, as was Julie Fiske Hogan, production coordinator of the *Fiske Guide to Colleges*. Cheryl Davis, Guy Hammond, and Jean Hammond also provided valuable editing assistance.

We are deeply indebted to our editors at Sourcebooks, including Todd Stocke, Peter Lynch, Carrie Obry, and Michelle Schoob whose enthusiasm for and dedication to the Fiske guides has been an inspiration. Also, thanks to Matt Diamond for his hard work on the design of this book.

College Counselors Advisory Group

Marilyn Albarelli, Moravian Academy (PA)
Scott Anderson, Mercersburg Academy (PA)
Christine Asmussen, St. Andrew's Sewanee School (TN)
Bruce Bailey, Lakeside School (WA)
Samuel Barnett, SchoolFutures (VA)
Amy E. Belstra, Cherry Creek H.S. (CO)
Greg Birk, Kinkaid School (TX)
Susan T. Bisson, Advocates for Human Potential (MA)
Robin Boren, Dakota Ridge H.S. (CO)
Clarice Boring, Cody H.S. (WY)
John B. Boshoven, Community High School & Jewish
    Academy of Metro Detroit (MI)
Mimi Bradley, St. Andrew's Episcopal School (MS)
Nancy Bryan, Pace Academy (GA)
Claire Cafaro, Ridgewood H.S. (NJ)
Jimmie Lee Cogburn, Woodward Academy (GA)
Nancy Caine, St. Augustine H.S. (CA)
Mary Calhoun, St. Cecilia Academy (TN)
Jane M. Catanzaro, College Advising Services (CT)

Mary Chapman, St. Catherine's School (VA)
Anthony L. Clay, Durham Academy (NC)
Kathy Cleaver, Durham Academy (NC)
Teresa A. Corrigan, Chapel Hill-Chauncy Hall School (MA)
Alison Cotten, Cypress Falls H.S. (TX)
Alice Cotti, Polytechnic School (CA)
Rod Cox, St. Johns Country Day School (FL)
Carroll K. Davis, North Central H.S. (IN)
Renee C. Davis, Rocky River H.S. (OH)
Mary Jo Dawson, Academy of the Sacred Heart (MI)
Christy Dillon, Crystal Springs Uplands School (CA)
Tara A. Dowling, Saint Stephen's Episcopal School (FL)
Lexi Eagles, American Hebrew Academy (NC)
Dan Feldhaus, Iolani School (HI)
Ralph S. Figueroa, Albuquerque Academy (NM)
Emily E. FitzHugh, The Gunnery (CT)
Larry Fletcher, Salesianum School (DE)
Nancy Fomby, Episcopal School of Dallas (TX)
Laura Johnson Frey, Vermont Academy (VT)
Phyllis Gill, Providence Day School (NC)

H. Scotte Gordon, Moses Brown School (RI)
Freida Gottsegen, Pace Academy (GA)
Molly Gotwals, Suffield Academy (CT)
Kathleen Barnes Grant, The Catlin Gabel School (OR)
Madelyn Gray, John Burroughs School (MO)
Amy Grieger, Northfield Mount Hermon School (MA)
Mimi Grossman, Saint Mary's Episcopal School (TN)
Elizabeth Hall, Education Consulting Services (TX)
Andrea L. Hays, The Bullis School (MD)
Rob Herald, Cairo American College (Egypt)
Darnell Heywood, Columbus School for Girls (OH)
Bruce Hunter, Rowland Hall St. Mark's School (UT)
Deanna L. Hunter, Shawnee Mission East H.S. (KS)
John Keyes, The Catlin Gabel School (OR)
Sharon Koenings, Brookfield Academy (WI)
Joan Jacobson, Shawnee Mission South H.S. (KS)
Diane Johnson, Lawrence Public Schools (NY)
Linda S. King, College Connections   (NY)
Gerimae Kleinman, Shaker Heights H.S. (OH)
Laurie Leftwich, Brother Martin H.S. (LA)
MaryJane London, Los Angeles Center for Enriched Studies
   (CA)
Martha Lyman, Deerfield Academy (MA)
Brad MacGowan, Newton North H.S. (MA)
Robert S. MacLellan, Jr., The Pingry School (NJ)

Margaret M. Man, La Pietra Hawaii School for Girls (HI)
Susan Marrs, The Seven Hills School (OH)
Karen A. Mason, Wyoming Seminary (PA)
Lisa Micele, University of Illinois Laboratory H.S. (IL)
Corky Miller-Strong, Culver Academies (IL)
Janet Miranda, Prestonwood Christian Academy (TX)
Richard Morey, Dwight-Englewood School (NJ)
Joyce Vining Morgan, Putney School (VT)
Daniel Murphy, The Urban School of San Francisco (CA)
Judith Nash, Highland H.S. (ID)
Deborah Robinson, Mandarin H.S. (FL)
Julie Rollins, Episcopal H.S. (TX)
William C. Rowe, Thomas Jefferson School (MO)
Bruce E. Scher, Chicagoland Jewish H.S. (IL)
David Schindel, Vail Mountain School (CO)
Kathy Z. Schmidt, St. Mary's Hall (TX)
Barbara Simmons, Bellarmine College Preparatory (CA)
Joe Stehno, Bishop Brady H.S. (NH)
Bruce Stempien, Weston H.S. (CT)
Paul M. Stoneham, The Key School (MD)
Audrey Threlkeld, Forest Ridge School of the Sacred Heart
   (WA)
Ted de Villafranca, Peddie School (NJ)
Scott White, Montclair H.S. (NJ)
Linda Zimring, Los Angeles Unified School District (CA)

NOTES

2006–2007 College Admission Calendar

January 2006
S	M	T	W	T	F	S
1	2	3	4	5	6	7
8	9	10	11	12	13	14
15	16	17	18	19	20	21
22	23	24	25	26	27	28
29	30	31				

February 2006
S	M	T	W	T	F	S
			1	2	3	4
5	6	7	8	9	10	11
12	13	14	15	16	17	18
19	20	21	22	23	24	25
26	27	28				

March 2006
S	M	T	W	T	F	S
			1	2	3	4
5	6	7	8	9	10	11
12	13	14	15	16	17	18
19	20	21	22	23	24	25
26	27	28	29	30	31	

April 2006
S	M	T	W	T	F	S
						1
2	3	4	5	6	7	8
9	10	11	12	13	14	15
16	17	18	19	20	21	22
23	24	25	26	27	28	29
30						

May 2006
S	M	T	W	T	F	S
	1	2	3	4	5	6
7	8	9	10	11	12	13
14	15	16	17	18	19	20
21	22	23	24	25	26	27
28	29	30	31			

June 2006
S	M	T	W	T	F	S
				1	2	3
4	5	6	7	8	9	10
11	12	13	14	15	16	17
18	19	20	21	22	23	24
25	26	27	28	29	30	

July 2006
S	M	T	W	T	F	S
						1
2	3	4	5	6	7	8
9	10	11	12	13	14	15
16	17	18	19	20	21	22
23	24	25	26	27	28	29
30	31					

August 2006
S	M	T	W	T	F	S
		1	2	3	4	5
6	7	8	9	10	11	12
13	14	15	16	17	18	19
20	21	22	23	24	25	26
27	28	29	30	31		

September 2006
S	M	T	W	T	F	S
					1	2
3	4	5	6	7	8	9
10	11	12	13	14	15	16
17	18	19	20	21	22	23
24	25	26	27	28	29	30

October 2006
S	M	T	W	T	F	S
1	2	3	4	5	6	7
8	9	10	11	12	13	14
15	16	17	18	19	20	21
22	23	24	25	26	27	28
29	30	31				

November 2006
S	M	T	W	T	F	S
			1	2	3	4
5	6	7	8	9	10	11
12	13	14	15	16	17	18
19	20	21	22	23	24	25
26	27	28	29	30		

December 2006
S	M	T	W	T	F	S
					1	2
3	4	5	6	7	8	9
10	11	12	13	14	15	16
17	18	19	20	21	22	23
24	25	26	27	28	29	30
31						

January 2007
S	M	T	W	T	F	S
	1	2	3	4	5	6
7	8	9	10	11	12	13
14	15	16	17	18	19	20
21	22	23	24	25	26	27
28	29	30	31			

February 2007
S	M	T	W	T	F	S
				1	2	3
4	5	6	7	8	9	10
11	12	13	14	15	16	17
18	19	20	21	22	23	24
25	26	27	28			

March 2007
S	M	T	W	T	F	S
				1	2	3
4	5	6	7	8	9	10
11	12	13	14	15	16	17
18	19	20	21	22	23	24
25	26	27	28	29	30	31

April 2007
S	M	T	W	T	F	S
1	2	3	4	5	6	7
8	9	10	11	12	13	14
15	16	17	18	19	20	21
22	23	24	25	26	27	28
29	30					